Nordic Walking for Total Fitness

Suzanne Nottingham

Alexandra Jurasin

Human Kinetics

Library of Congress Cataloging-in-Publication Data

Nottingham, Suzanne, 1958-
  Nordic walking for total fitness / Suzanne Nottingham and Alexandra Jurasin.
     p. cm.
  Includes bibliographical references and index.
  ISBN-13: 978-0-7360-8178-8 (soft cover)
  ISBN-10: 0-7360-8178-X (soft cover)
  1. Fitness walking. 2. Physical fitness. I. Jurasin, Alexandra, 1972- II.
Title.
  RA781.65.N68 2010
  613.7'176--dc22

                            2009033632

ISBN-10: 0-7360-8178-X (print)
ISBN-13: 978-0-7360-8178-8 (print)

The Web addresses cited in this text were current as of November 2009, unless otherwise noted.

Acquisitions Editor: Laurel Plotzke; **Developmental Editor:** Kevin Matz; **Assistant Editor:** Scott Hawkins; **Copyeditor:** Joy Wotherspoon; **Indexer:** Dan Connolly; **Permission Manager:** Martha Gullo; **Graphic Designer:** Fred Starbird; **Graphic Artist:** Kim McFarland; **Cover Designer:** Keith Blomberg; **Photographer (cover):** Eisend/Imago/Icon SMI; **Photographer (interior):** Neil Bernstein, unless otherwise noted; **Photo Asset Manager:** Laura Fitch; **Visual Production Assistant:** Joyce Brumfield; **Photo Production Manager:** Jason Allen; **Art Manager:** Kelly Hendren; **Associate Art Manager:** Alan L. Wilborn; **Illustrator:** Alan L. Wilborn; **Printer:** United Graphics

Our thanks to UC Davis for allowing us to photograph in the campus Arboretum.

Human Kinetics books are available at special discounts for bulk purchase. Special editions or book excerpts can also be created to specification. For details, contact the Special Sales Manager at Human Kinetics.

Printed in the United States of America   10   9   8   7   6   5   4   3   2   1

The paper in this book is certified under a sustainable forestry program.

Human Kinetics
Web site: www.HumanKinetics.com

United States: Human Kinetics
P.O. Box 5076
Champaign, IL 61825-5076
800-747-4457
e-mail: humank@hkusa.com

Canada: Human Kinetics
475 Devonshire Road Unit 100
Windsor, ON N8Y 2L5
800-465-7301 (in Canada only)
e-mail: info@hkcanada.com

Europe: Human Kinetics
107 Bradford Road
Stanningley
Leeds LS28 6AT, United Kingdom
+44 (0) 113 255 5665
e-mail: hk@hkeurope.com

Australia: Human Kinetics
57A Price Avenue
Lower Mitcham, South Australia 5062
08 8372 0999
e-mail: info@hkaustralia.com

New Zealand: Human Kinetics
P.O. Box 80
Torrens Park, South Australia 5062
0800 222 062
e-mail: info@hknewzealand.com

E4768

Nordic Walking for Total Fitness

Contents

Preface   vi

Acknowledgments   viii

PART I

Better Fitness With the Nordic Approach

1 Walking Plus: The Gym to Go   2

2 Gearing Up: The Right Equipment for You   9

3 Taking the First Steps: Poling, Posture, and Stride   22

4 Stepping Up: Variations for Cardio, Strength, and Power   37

5 Changing Pace: Variations for Balance, Coordination, Agility, and Flexibility   72

6 Stepping Out: Adapting to Different Terrain   98

7 Starting Up: Identifying the Workout for You   108

PART II

Nordic Walking Workouts

8 Short and Easy   126

9 Medium and Steady   133

10 Medium and Quick   139

11 Short and Fast   145

12 Long and Steady   151

13 Outdoor Circuit Training   157

PART III

Programming
for Long-Term Goals

14 Training for Cardio Health and Fitness 170

15 Targeting Total-Body Fitness   179

16 Cross-Training for Sports   186

17 Customizing Your Program   195

Index   203

About the Authors   207

Preface

As a lifelong skier, I've found that using poles for balance, stability, and rhythm is as natural as brushing my teeth. So, more than 10 years ago, I had no trouble adjusting to using walking poles for summer fitness. As an instructor, I'd seen miracle after miracle in folks who used poles to improve their walking. But it wasn't until I needed a total hip replacement that the real miracle happened.

I am a long-distance hiker; I can trek up and down Mt. Whitney (22 miles) in one day without poles. Just one experience with the poles made me realize what I had in my hands. Poles became part of the contents of my car trunk for use any time, any place. I used Nordic walking poles for fitness walks until my hip surgery. The poles turned out to be integral during recovery, allowing me to bear weight evenly on both legs much sooner than I would have if I'd used the archaic, spine-wrenching recovery tools currently recommended by doctors—the dreaded walker and cane.

As an athlete, I knew better than to hurry in recovery. So, I took my time, gradually increasing my walking speed. My first official walk 12 days postop was on a path that typically takes 20 minutes. I will always remember that walk because it took 2 hours!

My postsurgery objective was to trek Mt. Whitney again in a day hike. On July 7, 2004, two years to the day postop, I did it again, but this time with poles. After a wholesome mantra during the 11 miles up ("posture, level chin, relaxed traps, relaxed pace, endurance"), the mantra for the 11 miles back down ("cold beer, hot bath; cold beer, hot bath") resonated through my body. But what didn't resonate this time was a stitch of pain. This was my miracle. And to this day, still no pain. Considering the times when I couldn't walk for a week after a hike because of a hip disability, this time the hike was nothing—except time, patience, and symmetrical movements thanks to the poles.

This book is a result of dedication to the functional activity of Nordic walking. The Nordic Walk Now team trainers also devoted their expertise, passion, and time to this work; my coauthor, Alexandra Jurasin, and I are greatly appreciative of that. Since March 2006 we have worked to mesh science, skills, and innovation to bring our customers and readers the most updated information available about Nordic walking fitness.

The North American low-impact techniques described in this book are proprietary to Nordic Walk Now and fast becoming well known as the safest path to reaching the objectives of Nordic walking fitness. We believe that to prevent injuries, you must be aware of impact and how to avoid it with efficient technique and an attention to your own process of motor-skill development. The good news is that we walk you through it from point A to point Z. Our only goals for you are that you grasp Nordic walking in any way that fits into your regimen and choose it as one of your lifelong sports.

In this book, although similar principles and methods of athletic training are used, it is inappropriate to recommend longer pole lengths because we cannot assume that everyone is interested in training with the specificity or intensity of a professional athlete. Even more important is our conservative approach toward developing fitness proficiency. We won't assume you are at a certain fitness level. Instead, we provide the progressive path to "walk yourself into fitness" at any intensity that suits you. Furthermore, consider that pro athletes have trainers by their sides, have gone through extensive evaluation and testing, and have experience using poles. Finally, remember that you get out of Nordic walking what you put into it. This is the beauty of the sport. If you choose to walk slower, you will acquire strength, but with less resistance from the tips you will get a lower impact workout. If you choose to walk with speed and power, you'll acquire strength proportionate to your effort. In either case, you will walk stronger!

Acknowledgments

We thank our athlete models who danced for the camera with effortless grace: Courtney McElvain, Elisabeth Marsh, Michael Cohee, Alex Buss, and Jane Rackl. Special thanks to Kendra Densmore and her family for always being there with consistent support and belief in the cause from the start. My children Taylor and Lucas deserve special recognition over the past year for putting up so patiently with the words, "Sorry kids, I can't go out and play. I have to work on my book." Thanks to others who donated perspective and precious time: Debbie Chalfant, Rachael Clark, Christine Schnitzer, Jill Hall, Jennifer Lockwood, Kathy Freedlund, Rose Zahnn, Ken Alan, Linda Lemke, Janet Sheehan, Robin Barnes, Trish Alexander, and Jennifer Schweisinger. The generosity of our product sponsors is appreciated: SpringBoost, Thorlo, Leki, and Gabel. We also value the support of our peers in education: Malin Svensson of Nordic Walking North America, Tom Rutlin of Exerstrider, Dan Barrett of Fittrek, East Coast Alliance, and our friends at the American Council on Exercise. We give tremendous thanks to all the participants of our Nordic Walk Now instructor trainings over the last few years. Their participation, questions, and enthusiasm kept us learning and inspired to develop and teach a curriculum that extends beyond convention and touches everyone in profound ways. Finally, thanks to the University of California at Davis for allowing us to photograph the images in this book in the magnificent campus arboretum.

Better Fitness With the Nordic Approach

CHAPTER 1

Walking Plus:
The Gym to Go

Get outside and move forward! Imagine finally shedding that extra few pounds that many fitness programs fail to help you lose, completing your first half marathon, or relishing fitness in the splendor of the outdoors, away from walls, electronics, and the sweat of other people. What if you could do all this while increasing back strength and bone density? Nordic walking is a modern and complete method of full-body training. Through the workouts and programs provided in this book, we've created a system we call "gym to go," and it's a new form of cardio training—workouts guaranteed to help you accomplish the results you desire.

Nordic walking is a fitness activity that uses specially designed poles to engage the upper body's musculature. It offers a variety of benefits regardless of your fitness level, age, or experience. You can practice Nordic walking at almost any place and time, and it's free. The potential to improve your health and fitness level is right in the palms of your hands. You can start today and do it for the rest of your life. Add poles to the trunk of your car, and your gym is ready to go just about anywhere!

Nordic walkers combine poles and physical strength to move their own body weight forward and over the ground. This is how it provides both a cardio and strength workout simultaneously. The combination of continuous, rhythmic motion and the resistance generated by the tips of the poles creates powerful momentum. When body mass meets speed in one direction (in this case, forward), your reaction to resistance in the pole tips propels you forward.

You can create even more resistance by nailing the sweet spot of the tips every time. This practice is rhythmic automation at its best!

Advantages of Nordic Walking

Many benefits are associated with Nordic walking, including cardiorespiratory fitness, heart health, postural development, bone density, injury rehabilitation, pain management, muscle strength and endurance, mobility, stability, balance, and body awareness. Many fans call Nordic walking a "moving meditation," and say that it produces endorphins similar to those experienced in the runner's high. The long-term benefits for back health and weight loss that can be achieved by practicing Nordic walking at a leisurely pace are compelling, not to mention the fitness and athletic benefits gained from a faster, harder pace.

The practice is ageless and limitless. A good pair of poles costs between $59 and $200 US. After the initial investment of time to learn and money for poles, there is no further cost. You are free to wander the earth with the intensity that suits your objectives! Nordic walking is an investment in an athletic future that will help you stay active and fit throughout your golden years.

Health Benefits

Workouts may vary in intensity from slow, calculated walking to swift, heart-pumping paces, but every choice yields results. Everyone from grandmas to athletes can reap these benefits of Nordic walking, regardless of fitness level, ability, speed, or age.

Full-Body Fitness.   Nordic walking uses poles to connect the entire body to the pull of gravity, creating comprehensive muscle activity and resistance. With proper use, the tips of the poles redistribute the physical effort of your lower extremities to include your core and upper body.

Healthier Heart.   Nordic walking is a perfect cardiorespiratory activity for people at every fitness level. The benefits of Nordic walking are directly related to the amount of effort put forth; as your fitness level improves, you progressively reap greater benefits. As will be discussed, it is a perfect activity for enhancing cardiorespiratory stamina and strength.

Weight Loss.   Nordic walking results in greater weight loss than traditional walking does because more muscles are active, therefore burning more calories. However, when you are learning a new sport, your heart rate is sometimes too high to burn fat. Once you master the new skills and adapt to the demands of the activity, you can establish a fat-burning heart rate that helps you literally walk your butt off!

Healthier Back and Improved Posture.   Improving the health of your spine is a top reason for Nordic walking. Regardless of your knowledge and skill level, simply gripping the handles of the poles and touching their tips to the ground activates key postural muscles of your torso and core. One of the most beneficial results of tip resistance is spine rotation, which physical therapists prescribe as one of four daily movements for a healthy back. Rotational movements create gentle resistance around the axis of the spine, activating all the core muscles. By incorporating the rotational element that many fitness programs miss, Nordic walking reenergizes postural awareness. Better posture results in greater coordination, stronger back muscles, and increased endurance.

Reduced Impact on Joints.   Because poles distribute effort throughout the body and provide instant stability, Nordic walking places less strain on the knees and back. After only one trip uphill and downhill, you will appreciate the extent to which poles help you remain upright. Never again will you have to break at the waist or load your knees beyond a comfortable angle.

Greater Bone Density.   Avid Nordic walkers report stronger bones in all parts of the body.

Reduced Stress.   Nordic poles activate all the joints in the body, including the spine, causing the body to buzz with endorphins. Many Nordic walkers liken this feeling to the classic runner's high. Other benefits associated with increased endorphins include reduced stress, better pain management, and greater muscle endurance.

©Ingolf Pompe/Getty Images

Nordic walking can help reduce stress through its meditative qualities, but it can also be a great way to get a workout while visiting with friends.

Both Nordic walking and meditation draw the participant's awareness to rhythms, such as the heart's beat, the of breath, and the coordination of a symmetrical gait. Nordic walkers claim to lose track of time, letting the peaceful rush of rhythm and momentum occupy their minds throughout the workout. Others focus on one quality of their gait for several seconds at a time. Examples include noticing how their feet feel as each portion, from the heel to the toes, make contact with the ground, or concentrating on subtly coordinating the rotation of the upper and lower portions of the body.

Fitness and Athletic Benefits

Using Nordic walking poles requires coordinated movements for balance and stability, strength and endurance, varied cardiovascular efforts, agility and visual acuity. Added benefits include injury prevention, enhanced nervous system reactions to move quickly with precision, and the ability to learn and accomplish other sport skills in less time. The best health benefit is having a long, active life! To Nordic walk now is an investment in your athletic future to stay active into your golden years.

Cardiorespiratory Stamina.   Aerobic and anaerobic conditioning are at the core of the Nordic walking workout. Aerobic exercise utilizes readily available oxygen, glycogen, and fat stores to sustain movement and pace, most often at a consistent moderate heart rate, and it is performed for longer durations of time. Aerobic conditioning is the backbone of your training program, not just because it is inherent in a Nordic walking experience, rather because it preps your body for more intense anaerobic conditioning later on. Anaerobic activity requires a quicker source for energy, therefore instead of using fat stores, the main source of fuel is what is stored in your muscles, and what you ate for breakfast. It takes your heart rate to a new level of intensity that is often difficult to sustain longer than seconds or minutes. Because it is a distance exercise, Nordic walking is an endurance activity, working many of the muscle groups used in running and cross-country skiing. It is an ideal activity for cardiorespiratory fitness because it can be performed at any intensity. Also, those who wish to burn fat will have no trouble. Those who wish to compete at a higher level have options for intensive training. Others who simply wish to build a healthier heart or participate in sports can find the appropriate pace to suit their fitness goals.

Anaerobic conditioning takes your aerobic training to the next level. We think of anaerobic conditioning as advanced cardio training. Advanced cardiorespiratory activity increases both strength and power. The more intense your cardiac output is, the less readily oxygen is available to metabolize the fat that sustains energetic movement. Your body taps into other stores of quick energy for muscle function, such as what you ate for breakfast in addition to what you ate the day before that is stored as glycogen in your muscles. Your muscles cannot sustain the intense demands of this advanced cardio training for long. Instead, you should use interval training to progressively build your cardio machine.

Benefits of anaerobic conditioning or advanced cardio training include the following:

1. Healthier heart
2. Greater cardiorespiratory endurance
3. Increased fitness levels
4. Enhanced nerve response
5. Better dynamic balance
6. Faster recovery time
7. Greater speed
8. Improved performance in sports

Muscular Endurance. Muscular endurance is the ability to sustain movement or activity for a prolonged amount of time. With practice, skilled Nordic walkers acquire a more athletic gait that combines simultaneous physical reactions with a faster pace and speed. At this level of training, distance events become appealing and attainable. Muscular endurance allows you to settle into a comfortable yet productive pace.

Balance. Balance comes from bodily responses that maintain equilibrium. It is just as beneficial for mobility and body awareness as cardiovascular, strength, and flexibility. Everyone is born with balance, but savvy athletes know how to train to cultivate it. Some prefer a less strenuous approach to stability training, such as with the single-side balance exercise described in chapter 5. However, Nordic walking challenges you to achieve more dynamic balance because you are working the upper body to move forward while recovering small imbalances in the feet, ankles, legs, and pelvis. Poles challenge the upper and lower body simultaneously, resulting in better balance. Training for balance and becoming aware of the body's balance centers will help you attain superior motor efficiency and athletic ability. Remember that stability, mobility, and balance dance together at any intensity.

Range of Motion. Traditionally, power walkers use a shorter stride and an arm swing that often barely involves the upper body. These movements require less effort and use fewer muscles. Nordic walking techniques elicit a greater range of movement and a longer stride that activates more muscles and propels the body forward with strength. The pole action is an enhancement of the opposing arm swing used when walking normally. The increased range of motion allows you to literally cover more ground. Likewise, flexibility and other fitness qualities improve.

Agility. Agility relates to quickness and maneuverability. Starting or stopping suddenly, pivoting, dodging, jumping, and other types of fast footwork are skills that require muscle control. A variety of fun agility drills relate to

Nordic walking. Some involve the creative use of poles; others utilize the natural environment. Agility and balance work together to help you effortlessly adjust to stimulus that acts on your body to throw it off it's axis. Examples include impulsive direction changes or when you reach the top of a hill or run into a headwind. The body reacts to deflection to stabilize itself naturally. These athletic components are the prerequisites for coordination.

Coordination.   Coordination involves a complimentary relationship of movements—a smooth flow from one slight movement to the next to accomplish an efficient stride. You must move the upper and lower body both independently and in opposition. Rhythm and coordination determine pace, which can eventually equal speed. Although power may not always be required for Nordic walking, coordination is the most obvious athletic component. Your Nordic walking skills will be efficient when your movements are so subtle and well memorized that your brain is able to communicate instructions for movement with ease, developing physical and mental sequential reactions without wasting energy. Coordination training combines balance, agility, and visual skills. It can also include power training. Other activities like group exercise classes, sports, and eye-foot or eye-hand drills are also effective for developing coordination.

Efficiency of Movement.   Nordic walkers often comment that their practice helps them walk with greater grace and ease, even without poles. Nordic walking enhances both posture and coordination. Nordic walking poles lengthen the body's levers (the arms and legs as they swing in opposition) and its stride length (the distance between the feet). Efficiency of movement, or using as little energy as possible to accomplish skills, is both the result and objective of skilled Nordic walkers. Additional benefits include fewer injuries, better reaction time, quicker and more precise movement, and greater mastery of sport skills.

Visual Skills.   Balance and its recovery depend on visual cues. You need superior visual skills to hit a baseball, kick a soccer ball, and stay upright when your lightweight poles accidentally tangle in your legs during a high cross wind! Nordic walkers are fortunate because the stability created by the pole tips lets them focus their vision ahead instead of down at the ground. The practice of gazing ahead with a soft focus, taking in the entire landscape, is much healthier for the spine. If you continually look down at the ground, the placement of your head can injure your spine, pulling your shoulders and upper torso away from the center of the pelvis and the axis of efficiency. Over time, your bones may grow out of alignment. The visual skills gained during Nordic walking assist postural integrity by helping you appropriately balance your head's weight, improving poor posture and eliminating back strain. Adept vision also helps prevent needless injuries on crowded bike paths and on busy sidewalks.

Strength and Power.   Training for strength and power develops muscles that are controlled and responsive. Strength is the prerequisite for intense power training and injury prevention. Furthermore, it produces positive adaptations that improve balance, agility, and more. Coordinating simultaneous movements, like those in Nordic walking, requires full-body effort to support the demands of repetitive motion and endurance. If performed safely, a balanced strength program results in muscle balance and back health.

The result of a sound program of power conditioning is muscular involvement with a quality of explosive reaction. For example, competitive runners train with sprint drills to help them pick up the pace at the end of the race. Power training is appropriate for any type of endurance sport performed at a high level of proficiency. However, you must have developed your muscles with specific strength exercises that build structural integrity before beginning power conditioning. You must be strong enough to endure high-impact exercises and drills. Sprints, leaps, bounds, and skips are specific examples of Nordic walking drills. Other low-impact options for the whole body include performing power intervals on a slide board or a bike and training for core stability with a medicine ball. Power is strength plus speed combined; therefore, power drills reflect this explosive nature of exercise. You should not attempt a power-training regimen if you haven't already worked through a solid fitness program for several months or even years. If your goal is to train to Nordic walk a marathon, power training will help you prevent the injuries and excessive fatigue associated with long distances. It also gives you the aerobic capacity to sustain pace and the anaerobic power to surge ahead of the competition–an advantage that separates winners from losers in sports.

CHAPTER 2

Gearing Up:
The Right Equipment
for You

Most outdoor activities require gear, and Nordic walking is no exception. If you're a gear enthusiast, many brands of technical clothing and accessories provide options for exercising in cold or hot climates. However, if your athletic closet is already crammed with equipment, Nordic walking need not add much to the burden. In essence, all you need for Nordic walking is appropriate footwear and the definitive piece of equipment, a pair of poles.

This chapter discusses the variety, uses, and distinguishing features of poles that are manufactured for Nordic walking. They differ from poles for cross-country skiing, which are too long for Nordic walking, and poles for Alpine skiing and trekking, which are too heavy. Although some people believe that the poles for Nordic walking and trekking are interchangeable, they are designed very differently. Visualize poles used for hiking or trekking, which are similar to a mountain bike in that they are both tools for highly technical sports that involve twisting, turning, and going up and down extremely steep hills. Accordingly, the primary use of these tools is to enhance stability and balance on rugged trails. Trekking poles have swing weight built into the lower section to help you break through shrubs and difficult terrain while hiking. Trekkers plant their pole tips in front and to the sides of the body for stability and safety on the trail and while crossing streams.

Nordic walking poles are used in an opposite fashion. If trekking is like riding a mountain bike, Nordic walking is like riding a road bike. They are both classically aerobic activities, but have the potential for anaerobic training. Nordic walking poles are lighter, sleek, and streamlined for forward propulsion. The ideal terrain for Nordic walking is an open asphalt road or a dirt path at least 4 feet (1.2 m) wide, but you can also walk on gravel, sand, and grass. Another distinct difference in technique is that Nordic walkers keep their pole tips to the sides and behind the body to propel themselves forward and to achieve a cardiorespiratory workout.

Poles can range in price from $59 to $200. This chapter highlights the differences in design features of various models and compares Nordic walking poles to trekking poles in detail. It also addresses footwear, apparel, and optional accessories for Nordic walking.

Poles

Although they are simple, Nordic walking poles have distinguishing features that set them apart from poles used for skiing or trekking, as well as from other brands used for Nordic walking. The following section discusses the handle, wrist strap, shaft, and rubber tip in detail.

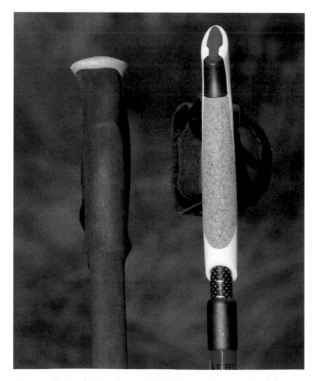

Figure 2.1   A Nordic walking pole's handle (right) versus a trekking pole's handle (left).

Handle   The handle, located at the top of the Nordic walking pole (figure 2.1), is one of the unique features of this piece of equipment. In contrast to trekking poles, which are thicker in diameter, most Nordic walking poles have a narrow profile. This sleek and purposeful design encourages you to hold the poles loosely, allowing them to float in your hands during movement.

Handles can be made of soft and shaped rubber, cork, or neoprene, depending on the model and manufacturer. Some walkers prefer cork, which is cooler to the touch in hot weather, and others prefer rubber or neoprene, which retain body heat in cooler weather.

Wrist Strap   Most poles have a wrist strap, which is attached to the handle approximately 1 inch (2.5 cm) below the top of the pole, and some are removeable by clicking out of a Nordic walking pole. Unlike the looping strap of trekking poles (figure 2.2a), the wrist strap conforms to the hand and passively attaches the wrist to the pole. In contrast, the looping straps on trekking poles require you to actively grip the handle. By design, the passive wrist strap (figure 2.2b) allows you to effortlessly move the pole with your hand while maintaining a neutral wrist. Wrist straps are usually constructed of soft, breathable material, and some models offer different sizes to ensure a glovelike fit.

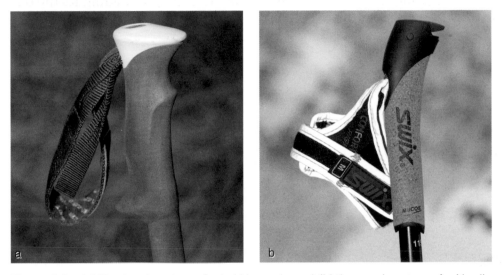

Figure 2.2   (a) The looping strap of a trekking pole and (b) the passive strap of a Nordic walking pole.

This unique design provides several benefits. For example, the passive hand contact around the pole handle reduces unnecessary activation of muscles in the wrist and forearm. Contracting smaller arm muscles often leads to over-activation of the neck and shoulders. Golfers know that hand contact around the club that results in gripping that is too tight wreaks havoc on an otherwise relaxed and accurate golf swing and leads to premature fatigue over the course of a game. Similarly, you should minimize unnecessary muscle tension, which causes inefficient movement, premature fatigue, and possible muscle strain. One of the many reported benefits of Nordic walking is the reduction of muscle tension in the neck and shoulders (Anttila et al. 1999, Karvonen et al, 2001), which also relieves the stress commonly held in that area of the body. Maintaining loose hand contact around the pole handle during exercise may decrease blood pressure from contracted muscles and encourage blood flow. Finally, individuals who cannot make tight hand contact around a pole due to arthritis or other conditions can still use the poles effectively.

Some wrist straps have a release button or trigger mechanism that detaches them from the pole. This convenient design allows you to easily sip a bottle of water or take off a jacket without removing the straps altogether. Choose the design of your poles according to your needs and your skill level.

Regardless of design, you should wear the wrist strap appropriately to minimize the risk of injury. With most designs, place your hand through the largest opening and your thumb through the smaller opening and tighten the Velcro strap around your wrist until the fit is snug but does not cause friction or hinder circulation. If your model has a removable wrist strap that offers multiple attachment settings, attach it as close to the handle as possible to reduce excessive movement between your wrist and the pole (figure 2.3).

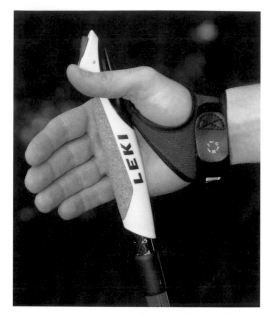

Figure 2.3   There are a variety of strap systems. Some poles come with removable straps, which can be a convenience to grab with. Regardless of the type, be sure the strap fits snugly.

Shaft   The pole shaft connects the handle with the tip, which makes contact with the ground. Like the poles used in trekking and skiing, the shafts of Nordic walking poles are made from a variety of alloys, including aluminum, carbon fiber, and fiberglass. To increase the efficiency of aerobic exercise, Nordic walking poles are light and have little swing weight, sometimes weighing as little as 13 ounces (370 g). Heavier swing weights are counterproductive for Nordic walking, since the poles' tips should remain behind the body to propel you forward. To minimize swing weight, some poles are designed so you can adjust the height at the top of the shaft.

The strong shafts of Nordic walking poles dampen vibration and absorb shock to ensure comfort, safety, durability, and efficiency. Materials that are too soft absorb your energy, but stiffer materials transfer kinetic energy to propel you forward. Nordic walking poles are also incredibly strong. One manufacturer, Leki, offers a lifetime warranty against breakage and states that their adjustable pole locking mechanism can withstand approximately 300 pounds (140 kg) of holding force.

Tips   Where the rubber meets the road, a uniquely designed tip clearly differentiates Nordic walking poles from other types of equipment. Trekking poles typically have hard and pointed metal tips or rounded rubber tips that are placed in front of the walker for support and balance. In contrast, Nordic walking poles have angled rubber tips (figure 2.4a) that propel you forward when placed on the ground behind you. This little rubber piece is special because it allows you to dictate the intensity of the workout by the amount of effort you apply to it, regardless of your speed.

Rubber tips vary in shape, length, and width. However, virtually all designs let you remove the tip to expose a sharper point for traction on softer and more varied terrain (figure 2.4*b*). The rubber tips are typically used for asphalt and cement and the heavy metal or tungsten carbide tips are used on dirt, grass, gravel, sand, and ice. You may determine which tip is most appropriate for you to avoid slipping. A few manufacturers now sell rubber tips that are embedded with carbide points. These models are designed for use on both hard and soft surfaces, including slick, wet surfaces and ice.

Like the tires on a car, rubber tips wear out over time. Replace them every six months for heavy use and once a year for moderate use. Replacement tips cost between $7 and $20.

Figure 2.4   *(a)* A pole with a rubber tip attached for walking on pavement and *(b)* with the rubber tip removed for walking on dirt and other off-road surface conditions.

Baskets   The small rubber baskets at the base of Nordic walking poles prevent the tips from bending or breaking in soft ground or gravel. Some manufacturers also offer an interchangeable webbed basket for use in the snow that costs between $8 and $25.

Pole Length: Fixed or Adjustable?

Depending on the brand you select, the length of Nordic walking poles is either fixed or adjustable. The following section discusses the pros and cons of each type to help you make an educated selection.

Most manufacturers offer Nordic walking poles of adjustable length. Both types have certain advantages. Some argue that fixed-length poles are lighter and quieter because they don't have heavy moving parts or rattling hinges. Others purport that fixed-length poles are stronger and therefore safer. Fixed-length poles are typically less expensive than adjustable ones. Additionally, some walkers feel that they are easier to use.

Although some models of adjustable poles may be cumbersome, telescoping poles made from materials such as carbon fiber are often as light and as quiet as fixed-length poles and can weigh between 7 and 9 ounces. As previously mentioned, an adjustable pole can accommodate up to approximately 300 pounds (140 kg), depending on the manufacturer. This weight limit should be more than sufficient for Nordic walking, particularly since the poles are used more for pushing off the ground in pulses than for bearing weight. Unless the equipment is being used for pole vaulting, most poles should provide more than enough support for a Nordic walker!

Assuming that adjustable poles are equal to those of fixed length in terms of strength and weight, there are several other advantages. First, you can alter an adjustable pole to accommodate your advances in skill level over time. Beginning Nordic walkers tend to start with shorter poles, and may increase the length as they become more proficient or for use on varying terrain. For example, walking up and down hills, in sand, or in grass can require tiny adjustments. You may even decide to change the height of your poles depending on which shoes you're wearing. Additionally, multiple users of different heights can share adjustable poles. An obvious downside to this option is that users who share poles cannot walk together at the same time, benefiting from the social nature of the activity. Finally, adjustable poles are more travel-friendly because they can be stowed more readily. Some pole models have two adjustable points, which allows them to compress to fit into a suitcase. Be forewarned; do not attempt to pack your poles in your carry-on luggage. They may be confiscated by security, which is a bit more painful than losing a set of nail clippers. However, if you follow the rules and check them with your baggage, traveling with poles is a great option to ensure that your vacations include Nordic walking.

Pole Height: How Tall

Determining the best pole height is not an exact science. Some manufacturers determine pole height by simply calculating a fraction of body height. This is the easiest method, particularly if you are purchasing poles online. Other factors include the length of your arms and legs, stride length, joint mobility, technique, shoes, and terrain. Therefore, adjustable poles help compensate for these other factors over time.

The following section outlines the mathematical calculation for determining pole height. Many experts recommend that pole height be roughly 68 percent of body height. Most manufacturers sell poles measured in centimeters, so readers who don't use the metric system should use the following calculations to estimate pole height:

$$\text{Walker's height (inches)} \times 2.54 = \text{Walker's height (cm)}$$

$$\text{Walker's height (cm)} \times 0.685 = \text{Estimated pole height (cm)}$$

If your poles are measured in inches, simply multiply your body height in inches by 0.685 to estimate the necessary pole height.

The following method more accurately accounts for limb length, and must be done with a set of poles in hand:

1. Loosen poles until they reach a height that is slightly higher than your chest.
2. Place your hand through the strap and tighten it.
3. Place the rubber tips next to your heels.
4. Relax your shoulders and your hand contact around the handles (wrist should be neutral), extend your arms in front of your body, and lower your hands until your wrists are slightly lower than your elbows or at the level of your navel.
5. As the poles gently glide to the correct height, mentally mark the desired pole height. Then, place the pole on the ground. Lift the pole you are going to adjust at an angle between vertical and horizontal and tighten it accordingly. Match the other pole's height to the adjusted one and tighten accordingly.

This method also considers the length of your arm when extended. If it is maintained during exercise, arm extension can increase range of motion in the shoulder joint and can subsequently involve more muscles. It is also the key to using the poles optimally and efficiently.

You must use poles of the proper height to prevent injury. Generally speaking, if you are unsure of proper technique, use shorter poles to accommodate your shorter strides and limited range of motion in your trunk, shoulders, and arms. Tall poles may force longer stride lengths and greater range of motion than you are ready for. Beginners in any fitness activity tend to do too much too soon, which may result in injury. As you advance you will need longer poles, and adjustable poles facilitate correct sizing.

Modifying the pole length is beneficial for accommodating the heights of different shoes, varied terrain, and changes in skill level. This can only be done with adjustable poles. Shorten your pole approximately 1 inch (2.5 cm) when walking on dirt trails, uneven surfaces, or inclines to allow the poles to move more freely. You should also shorten your poles a bit if you have preexisting injuries. Lengthen the poles as your stride length and upper-body flexibility increase. Although these adjustments may seem minor, small nuances in biomechanics can determine whether your movement is inefficient or fluid.

Pole Maintenance

Nordic walking poles require very little maintenance. If you have fixed-length poles, your only concern is cleaning. If you have adjustable poles, consult both the sections on cleaning and pole separation.

Cleaning

One of the unfortunate by-products of outdoor exercise is that gear can get quite dirty when exposed to the elements. Who bounds into the garage excited to clean gear after an intense workout or a day outdoors? Fortunately, you won't need to clean your poles very often.

The parts of the pole that have the most contact with grime and sweat are the handle and the wrist strap. Wipe down the handle with a damp cloth after each use. Gently wash the wrist strap with warm water and mild soap, and then blot it dry with a towel.

After walking in snow or rain, you should wipe off the pole shafts with a dry cloth. If you use adjustable poles in really wet conditions, separate the two parts of the shaft and set them out to dry. On the other hand, after walking in sand or on dirt trails, use a damp cloth to wipe off the poles and restore their look to new. If you adjust your poles regularly, you should clean the shafts to keep dirt or debris out of their locking mechanisms.

The bottom tip of the pole has plenty of opportunities to get dirty. Keeping the grooves in the rubber tip clean may give you better traction on cement or asphalt. After using the poles on a dirt trail or in the sand, wipe the exposed surface of the tip completely with a damp cloth. If you really like to keep your equipment pristine, you may remove the rubber tips from the poles and rinse them with water. If you have difficulty removing the tips, put a small amount of baby powder inside them and make sure they are clean before you put them back on the poles.

Pole Separation

This section applies only to adjustable poles. You may need to separate the different sections of your poles to clean them or to repair any complications with the tightening mechanism. Although brands differ in design, the following directions can be used for most styles of adjustable poles.

First, as a precaution, hold the poles nearly vertical whenever handling them or making adjustments. Those standing next to you will appreciate this safety tactic, because if you chose to pull the shaft apart horizontally, you might inadvertently jab them when the pole releases. Next, use your nondominant hand to grasp the upper shaft just above the adjustment point and your dominant hand to grasp the lower shaft. Holding the pole stable with your nondominant hand, use your dominant hand to loosen the lower section by rotating it to the left. Use the adage "righty tighty, lefty loosey" to remember the directions for loosening and tightening. Once you feel some give between the two sections, firmly pull them apart.

The lower shaft of most brands has a plastic device at the top called the *expander,* which tightens the pole and locks the two shafts together. Occasionally, the expander may become stuck, making it difficult to tighten or loosen the pole. In this case, turn the expander until it appears to be in a middle position, then place the top shaft over the lower shaft and push the two sections together. Use your nondominant hand to hold the pole by the top shaft in a nearly vertical position, and then turn the bottom shaft to the right with your dominant hand. Most styles of poles are sensitive to overtightening. Usually, a few complete revolutions of the lower shaft are sufficient to tighten the sections back together.

Shoes

As in any form of exercise, you need proper footwear to enjoy activity, perform well, and prevent injuries. Gravity and motion place an enormous amount of stress on your feet. Many people trust appearances to convey the lifespan of their shoes, but they can be misleading because the shoes' support and capacity for shock absorption decline long before their aesthetics do. As a general rule, athletic shoes significantly lose their ability to provide support and absorb shock after 500 miles (805 km). At this rate, if you walk approximately 3 miles (5 km) per day, three to four days a week, you will need a new pair of shoes every year. Since athletic shoes provide the foundation for all of your biomechanical movements and absorb the forces of gravity, they are not an accessory you should skimp on. There's nothing like a new pair of shoes to put a spring in your step and give you a renewed sense of energy, so do the right thing and protect your feet with high-quality shoes. Until recently, shoes specifically made for Nordic walking did not exist in the United States. A few shoe manufacturers, such as SpringBoost, Reebok, and Lowa, make models for Nordic walking that range in price from $70 to $200. The general design focuses on support in the heel and flexibility in the front. Some models have additional cushion and rugged outer soles for trail walking. Some are even waterproof. One particular model has a unique design that places the heel below the front of the foot for dorsiflexion (figure 2.6). The manufacturer purports that this shoe improves posture, balance, strength, and explosiveness. To choose the best shoe for you, determine the terrain and weather patterns of your walking area. For example, if you will be walking in wet weather, you should consider a waterproof shoe. If you plan to Nordic walk on dirt trails or uneven surfaces, you may want to select a shoe of a darker color that has deeper and stickier soles.

If you cannot find your shoe of choice at your local store, check the manufacturer's Web site.

If you cannot find a shoe that is specially designed for Nordic walking, you can buy another style that enhances your activity. Since Nordic walking is biomechanically different from running, a running shoe is not your best bet. If you are planning to walk predominantly on paved streets and sidewalks, choose a standard walking shoe. However, if you wish to Nordic

Figure 2.6 Nordic walking shoes are designed to aid forward propulsion when Nordic walking.

walk on dirt trails, select a hiking shoe with a rubber sole. A good athletic walking shoe has many of the design characteristics of a Nordic walking shoe, including the following:

- *Heel support and cushion.* Unlike runners, walkers first make ground contact with their heels. Therefore, the heel of the shoe should have sufficient padding to absorb the force and a low profile to enhance stability.
- *Flexible forefront.* During push-off, walkers flex their toes twice as much as runners do. The front of the shoe must be flexible.
- *Spacious toe box.* The front of the shoe should also be wide to accommodate the spread of the toes during the forceful push-off.

Ultimately, individual preference is the final deciding factor. Since every walker has unique anatomical and biomechanical characteristics, shoe selection is personal. Try on and test out as many pairs as you possibly can to make a good decision. For a custom fit, you may also want to purchase supportive insoles or see a podiatrist. Superfeet insoles are tailored for walking shoes to stabilize the foot, assist with temperature control, provide cushioning, and minimize pain. Heel pain and plantar fasciitis may develop with inadequate support, excessive activity, or even a change in activity. Again, you must have shoes that fit properly and support your feet in order to enjoy the exercise and prevent injury. Although most soft-soled shoes don't require as much time to break in, you should incorporate your new shoes into your routine slowly rather than wearing them for the first time on a 10-mile (16-km) walk. The hot spots and undue pain which may ensue are every athlete's nemesis.

Apparel

Although the fresh air, peaceful surroundings, and natural beauty you encounter in outdoor workouts are wonderful, the exposure to the elements can create extra demands on your body. Before venturing outdoors, you must plan ahead for safety by wearing appropriate clothing and bringing necessary supplies.

Once you have selected proper shoes, you should next look for a good pair of socks. Since your feet sweat, keeping them dry is of paramount importance for comfort and for minimizing hot spots and blisters. Brands of wool socks such as SmartWool provide exceptional comfort, wick moisture away from the skin, and are not itchy. Socks made of polyester and nylon, such as Thorlos, have similar wicking benefits. In addition to keeping your feet dry, these socks typically feature reinforced padding in the heel, arch, or ball of the foot for extra comfort.

Once you have taken care of your feet, turn your attention to your clothing.Selecting proper clothing is critical, particularly when exercising in environments with extreme temperatures and humidity. Your body moderates temperature with sweat, which cools you off as it evaporates. When buying exercise clothing that you wear next to your skin, choose items made from material that moves sweat away from the body so it can evaporate more quickly. Clothing technology has advanced in recent years, providing plenty of options for the outdoor exerciser. When selecting athletic clothing, choose items without seams that may cause discomfort or chafing. Fabrics that breathe, wick moisture, and insulate the body are key for comfort and performance. Fabric such as Coolmax move moisture away from the skin at twice the speed of cotton, which keeps body temperature constant whether it is hot or cold outside. Newer polyester blends incorporate silver dioxide, which has anti-bacterial properties, and titanium oxide, which protects against UVA and UVB radiation into the fabric. Compression wear, or tight-fitting pieces for the upper and lower body, may enhance performance by supporting and aligning the muscles, which increases oxygenation, circulation, and power and minimizes muscle soreness.

If you plan to walk in wind or rain, you should wear a second layer of clothing. Pants and jackets that are lightweight and either water resistant or waterproof allow you to maintain your body temperature in spite of the elements. Look for materials that let your skin breathe and keep moisture away from the body. Clothing that is not permeable to moisture traps your sweat next to the skin, causing you to overheat. Newer designs can also protect you from insects. Most stores that provide gear for hiking and running will stock clothing that works well for Nordic walking.

If you plan to walk when the conditions are overcast, warm, or hot, wear a hat with a wide brim to regulate your body temperature and protect your head, neck, and face from sun damage. When the weather is cold, choose tight caps that hold heat in or headbands that cover your ears.

Finally, you may want to protect your hands with gloves regardless of the weather. Even in warm weather, the padding of fingerless gloves provides additional comfort with the pole strap (figure 2.7). Full-length gloves made from materials that insulate and breathe can provide comfort in cold weather.

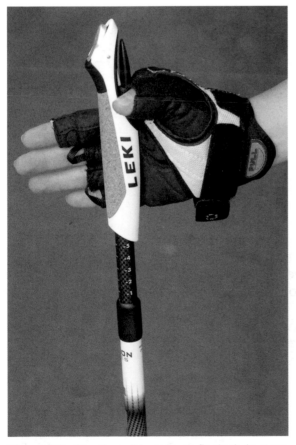

Figure 2.7 Nordic walking gloves fit nicely in most strap systems.

Pedometers, Heart Rate Monitors, and Other Accessories

In addition to clothing, you should consider several other items when going for both short and long hikes. Since hydration is essential, you can conveniently carry water or electrolyte drinks with a water bottle clip or belt pack around your waist. Consider carrying a backpack for items such as clothing, snacks, car keys, cell phone, identification, and contact information in case of an emergency. If you enjoy rhythmic walking, or are just inspired by music, you can easily carry an MP3 player in a case that fits on a belt or an armband.

For tracking performance, consider carrying a pedometer, a GPS, or a heart rate monitor. A lot of emphasis has been placed on pedometers in recent years, due to the 10,000 steps a day awareness campaign first inspired by the U.S. Surgeon General's recommendation to increase daily activity to at least 30 minutes a day. At 2,000 steps per mile, the program goals are meant to encourage individuals to walk 5 miles a day which will help surpass the Surgeon General's guidelines. Worn on the waist, pedometers measure vertical acceleration of the body which can be detected when each step is taken. They can be a great,

Heart rate monitors are a great way of tracking performance.

inexpensive tool that is lightweight and easy to use; however, they are typically more reliable for faster walking and running paces. They are unable to detect changes in walking speed since stride length is typically pre-set, but they appear to function equally good on various types of terrain. Pedometers range in price from $5-$90, where the more expensive models are included on a watch with a heart rate monitor. Many of them calculate total mileage, speed, and even caloric expenditure although this feature has not been shown to be a valid measure.

On the other hand, accelerometers are an emerging fitness tool that takes the pedometer one step further. Because they measure both acceleration and deceleration proportional to muscular force, they can more accurately detect caloric expenditure, although the strongest correlation for caloric estimates is still through the use of heart rate. A nice feature of accelerometers is that they can be worn on the waist or the limbs, as has been seen with manufacturers such as Nike who place the accelerometer on the wrist or conveniently within the heel of their shoes. Another advantage of the device is that it can detect changes in intensity and provide more accurate information for some one who is varying their workout speeds within the routine. For these reasons, they are typically the most objective and detailed physical activity data sources for research purposes to date. However, accelerometers typically only record a single plane of movement; therefore, they are not ideal for cycling, swimming, or weight lifting. Similar to pedometers, they can record time and speed, and are often are coupled with other technology on the device such as a heart rate monitor and range in prices from $40-$200 for commercial models.

If you want to track your mileage most accurately, the more recent wristband GPS devices are not only sleeker, but they track virtually any metric you can possibly be interested in including: location, distance, time, altitude, temperature, calories, and heart rate as well. Watch style GPS devices manufactured by brands such as Garmin and Suunto typically range from $150-$300. If you are not interested in all of those options and only want to focus on heart rate, there are a myriad of heart rate monitor options at price points ranging from $50-$250. One of the most prominent heart rate monitor brands is Polar. Price differences account for the ability to not only measure heart rate, but track target heart rate zones, and caloric expenditure with the more sophisticated models having download capabilities to report trends over time for long-term training goals.

References

Anttila, Holopainen, and Jokinen. 1999. Polewalking and the effect of regular 12-week polewalking exercise on neck and shoulder symptoms, the mobility of the cervical and thoracic spine and aerobic capacity. *Final project work for the Helsinki IV College for health care professionals.*

Karvonen, Mörsky, Tolppala, and Varis. 2001. The effects of stick walking on neck and shoulder pain in office workers. *Final project work at Mikkeli Polytechnic School. Degree programme of Physiotherapy.*

CHAPTER **3**

Taking the First Steps:
Poling, Posture, and Stride

Considering you've been walking for most of your life, how tough can Nordic walking be? Beginners often comment that learning is a bit harder than they had expected. Nordic walking requires longer movements of the arms and legs than classic power walking does. You're also learning to deal with unfamiliar equipment. This chapter teaches you to use your equipment effectively and efficiently to prevent injuries. Skill progressions serve as stepping stones to help you safely and comfortably improve your technique. Some people learn to Nordic walk very quickly and others don't. Acquiring this new set of skills takes practice, regardless of your fitness level.

A low-impact approach to conditioning is the safest way to learn Nordic walking without injuring your knees and rotator cuffs. Repetitive-use injuries are common with high-impact techniques that advocate tightly gripping the handles, lifting the poles off the ground, and planting the pole tips with intentional force. This chapter explains proper use of the equipment, specifically the rubber tips, which are your tools for strength training and resistance. When you use the new piece of strength-training equipment, work on your form before adding resistance. Once you've learned form and technique for Nordic walking, you can safely add tip resistance to take your training objectives to new levels, including specific cardiorespiratory training, strength, agility, and power.

Given that Nordic walking was originally created as dry-land training for cross-country skiers, some obvious similarities exist between the two sports. Both enhance the body's natural patterns of movement for walking, running, and skating. They are cardiorespiratory in nature and improve posture. Some of the skills of cross-country skiing do crossover to Nordic walking, but the physics, biomechanics, and skill sets are different because there is no glide time like on snow. The advantage of Nordic walking is that you can practice it throughout the year.

In spite of bad habits, over time, people develop the bodily awareness to sit, stand, and move with efficiency. Many people have lost the natural ability to swing their arms and legs in opposition as they walk. Some people have never learned about posture, walking technique, or seated ergonomics. Others have experienced physical challenges, such as injury or illness, which affect their movements. As a result, the area around the torso and pelvis locks, creating a tremendous muscle imbalance that changes the bone structure of the spine. Some move from the elbows and knees (instead of from the shoulders and hips), failing to rotate the torso or pelvis.

Physical therapists often recommend Nordic walking for loosening up the upper back, torso, and pelvis. Nordic walking builds the structure for a natural and symmetrical gait, helping you improve your posture, muscle balance, core strength, heart function, weight, athletic ability, and overall fitness. Nordic walkers often comment that the techniques bring rhythm and coordination to their normal walking patterns.

Proper pole height is very important in order to correctly use the equipment and prevent injury. See chapter 2 for instructions on determining the correct pole height. Especially for beginners, poles that are too long keep you from fully extending your arms, negatively affecting your shoulders and back. Adjust your poles to the proper height before beginning.

An efficient Nordic walking stride includes relaxed and natural gait in which the arms and legs move in comfortable opposition. As their swing increases, so does the stride length. Practice helps you create resistance with an efficient arm swing that allows optimal contact of the pole tips to the ground.

Choose an area for walking that is free of traffic. You need a space at least 4 feet (1.2 m) wide to accomplish a stride for moderate fitness. If you are walking with others, be respectful of personal space. Your poles can get tangled with your neighbor's if you walk too close together! Chapter 6 provides more details about selecting the proper outdoor environment.

Skill Development and Injury Prevention

The American College of Sports Medicine (ACSM) recommendations for healthy activity and training define injury prevention as the highest quality of any fitness program. Most Nordic walking injuries are due to repetitive use, or repeated jarring, of the shoulders and rotator cuffs. These upper-body injuries happen over time with use of inefficient techniques that produce impact. Rolling through the length of the feet creates less impact for the lower body. Other injuries include bruises and contusions due to carelessness.

You can avoid injury with a combination of knowledge of technical skills and of the body's learning process. When you begin a new activity or sport, you often attempt to recreate the skill. When you learn sequentially, your skills are positional, as in a still photograph, rather than dynamic, as in a movie. At first, you need to think through the learning process. This book teaches techniques sequentially, or one at a time, to give you time to acquire the skills appropriately. However, you don't need to think as much as your execution becomes more automatic. Practice results in a dynamic blend of skills. In Nordic walking, this can take anywhere from 8 to 80 practice sessions!

When learning remains sequential, movements eventually become contrived and unrealistic. This happens when walkers fail to see movement and skills as a dynamic continuum. An example of a contrived skill is the release of the poles. Classic Nordic walking techniques mimic cross-country skiing. Still photographs often show the hand releasing the pole well behind the body. However, if an average person attempts this technique with Nordic walking poles, the movements are often forced and unsuccessful. This process is based on a perception, perhaps one of a motionless image, like a snapshot, of "good" technique rather than in the reality of the dynamic needs of Nordic walking. There is nothing flowing or dynamic about this type of effort. Nordic walking movements should feel natural.

The opposite technique involves economy of motion, in which you learn to move only as necessary to accomplish the skills. You adapt to the physical demands instead of trying to plan out your load. The best skiers use economy of motion, moving only to adjust their balance. This principle is as important for athletes doing high-intensity training as it is for elderly people who simply wish to walk around the block.

As you explore Nordic walking, remember that no single technique works for everyone! For example, very skilled Nordic walkers can accomplish a classic cross-country pole release mostly during the high-intensity drills like bounding which takes the place of the "glide" in cross-country skiing allowing enough time for the release to take place. However, most people will never reach that level of biomechanical ability. The best techniques help you feel successful right away, regardless of your limitations. If you're having a hard time grasping the methods of Nordic walking, you need more information, better information, or more practice.

Pace is important because it affects how quickly your skill develops. At first, your pace is gradual while you slow movements down to effectively learn skills. With practice, your stride length will increase, working the muscles of the feet, ankles, and lower legs with deliberate movements. If you have done fitness walking for a long time, you may try to perform the foot speed and tempo of the power walk, which feels awkward combined with the longer levers of Nordic walking. This technique is unnatural. Instead, practice a calm and consistent cadence. Your objective in Nordic walking is to be coordinated, rhythmical, graceful, elegant, and powerful.

Remember that even if you pick up the techniques quickly, you must still take time to change the movement patterns you've been practicing your entire life. This process usually takes eight weeks. Changing too much and too soon injures muscles, connective tissues, and nerves. Imagine doing a long series of very high kicks, like the cancan. When was the last time you did high kicks? Most people would say never, or that it's been a long time. Trying the cancan would likely result in some kind of ankle, groin, or back injury because your body does not have the flexibility or strength to sustain that type of movement without momentum. You will get similar results if you try to change your stride length from 13 to 15 inches (33-38 cm) overnight. Your training progression starts with skill development. This chapter provides an eight-week program to aid your progress.

Technique Progressions

Give your body enough time to adapt to new loads and moving with longer levers by learning in a progression. The following techniques are presented in the order in which they should be practiced. Eventually, these skills will become more automatic, with one blending smoothly into the next. If you start noticing small mistakes, like lack of coordination or bouncing the tips, refer back to these skills. It is likely that you've missed a step. Together, these skills create an efficient Nordic walking technique that keeps you free of injury. The following workout gives you eight weeks to get into your Nordic walking groove!

Progressions for Upper-Body Technique: Poling and Posture

The first thing you may notice about Nordic walking is how upright and relaxed the posture is (figure 3.1). This is because tip contact stimulates postural muscles. Efficiently connecting the rubber tips with the walking surface requires a lot of practice. However, once those tips make contact, resistance is carried from the ground to your body through the poles, activating the primary postural muscles of the back and core!

Figure 3.1 Nordic walking requires an upright and relaxed posture.

As you'll learn, your primary focus when first learning upper body skills is not tip contact. As my golf instructor always says, "Focus on your swing and forget the ball!" Similarly, forget about the rubber tip, focusing instead on swinging the arm from the shoulder and the pole to find the sweet spot and engage the tips! The swing of the arm originates at the shoulder, carrying the hand and pole as it moves forward (figure 3.2). Many beginners assume they are supposed to lift and "place" the tips on the surface. This is an incorrect assumption—with proper technique via the one arm swing, the tips automatically aeroplane to the optimal spot on the surface. Long Arms is the second of eight basic skills that help you glide the tips along the walking surface.

Along with excellent posture, another noticeable quality of good Nordic walking is the effortless flow of the shoulders, arms, hands, and poles. The pole swing is an enhancement of normal arm movement for walking. Think of your arms as elongated bananas that maintain a slight elbow flex as they move in opposition to the legs. The pole tips propel the body's weight forward by pushing from behind.

The Nordic walking stride is completed with upper-body alignment. For successful striding, balance your head over your shoulders and keep your chin level with the walking surface. Focus your eyes ahead. Balance your shoulders over the pelvis for a strong base of support. Relax and elongate your shoulders and arms. Gently cup the poles' handles to keep the wrists aligned in neutral (figure 3.3).

Figure 3.2   The movements of the arms are like long levers, and the head should be balanced over the shoulders with the chin level with the walking surface.

Figure 3.3   Relax the shoulders and elongate the arms while keeping your wrists in a neutral position.

Once you can travel with speed and a wider stride, attempt to passively release the handle as your hand moves past your hip. However, if you are not travelling with sufficient velocity, you will not have enough time for the release. As you relax your grip at your hip, feel how your arm naturally lengthens as you walk forward to maintain tip contact for as long as possible. As a drill, some experienced Nordic walkers try to form a continuous line of the pole and arm.

Technique Progression 1: Walk and Swing

Rediscover the qualities of a natural gait. Walk and Swing gives you time to feel the oppositional long lever movements of the legs and arms as they swing, and to feel the location of the swings. Instructors refer back to Walk and Swing more than any other skill. If you do not have an awareness of oppositional movement, you will have difficulty mastering all the other skills.

1. Before beginning to walk, draw your awareness to your posture. Stand upright *(a)*.
2. Begin walking slowly on a flat, paved surface, as if you were strolling on the beach. Your stride should feel slower at first *(b)*.
3. Let go of your poles. Forget they are hanging from your wrists, forget the tips and do not be concerned if they are dragging at first. That will disappear with practice.
4. Use this time to become aware of the oppositional movement of your arms and legs. Work on feeling rhythmical, coordinated, and somewhat automated.
5. Try not to look down at the ground. Instead, hold your chin level with the walking surface. This practice appropriately balances the head's weight to maintain excellent posture and promote lower-back health.

Technique Progression 2: Long Arms

The purpose of this skill progression is to build your motor-skill memory for arm movement during forward propulsion with Nordic walking poles. Until now, your arm levers have been short during running or walking. The arm pumps more quickly for traditional power walking, which therefore shortens the stride length. This drill moves at a slower, lankier tempo. Acquiring this skill is the key to mastering all other Nordic walking skills.

1. Extend your arm as if to shake someone's hand. This is the appropriate length for Long Arms.

2. Recognize that in a natural gait, your arms swing to and fro. Half the swing takes place in front of the body, and the other half occurs behind it. But, Nordic walking requires lots more forward movement and much less back swing—hardly any, in fact!

3. At first, concentrate only on the forward movement of your arm. The arm swings farther in front, finishing its swing as it passes the hip.

4. As your hand and pole follow your arm, your hand should move no higher than your navel. Lower your hands and relax your shoulders!

5. At this point of your skill development, you may start to notice an increase in leg length and torso rotation.

Technique Progression 3: Cupping for Grip Development

Once you have established oppositional aware-ness and longer arms, develop a better relation-ship with the pole handles. The most efficient way to hold the pole handles is to cup them, using relaxed effort to guide the poles. As you practice, you may develop several inefficient movements of the hand and wrists, which are discussed later in the chapter (see the section on common errors on page 34).

1. Rest the pole handle in the middle of your palm.
2. Wrap your thumb gently around your fore-finger to create a light bond.
3. Lightly wrap the remaining fingers around the pole. Cupping the poles allows you more control during forward propulsion.

Technique Progressions for the Lower Body: Stride Length and Walking Mechanics

Almost instantly after beginning Nordic walking, you can feel your lower body change its movements to match the long levers of the upper body. In motor-skill development, leg movement tends to follow arm movement. Try walking with long arms and a short, quick stride. Or try the opposite, walking with bent elbows and long legs. Neither process feels like a natural effort.

Figure 3.4 For the Nordic walking stride, the heel of your lead foot should gently meet the ground as your opposite arm and hand swing forward from your shoulder.

Your lead leg should move forward from the hip. The heel of your lead foot should gently meet the ground as your opposite arm and hand swing forward from your shoulder (figure 3.4). The pole tip should make contact with the ground somewhere between the opposite heel and the middle of your stride distance between the feet. Flex the foot and roll it along the ground from the heel to toes, then swing the other leg through. In order to make technical progress, your Nordic walking stride length should be longer than your typical walking stride.

Technique Progression 4: Long Legs

Focusing on extending the leg from the hip and making efficient contact between the foot and the walking surface reduces impact on the lower body. The feet and lower legs become alive with sensation. Reduce impact by rolling the whole foot along the ground with each stride. This practice helps your knees and lower legs cushion surface contact and stimulates key muscles of the lower body that are responsible for balance and stability.

1. Start slowly with Walk and Swing to establish opposition. Become aware of your legs swinging forward from the hips.
2. Now bring attention to your feet and ankles. The most efficient strides utilize the entire foot. Your foot makes first contact by gently touching the heel to the ground, then rolls, touching each portion to the walking surface. As the toes make contact, use them to push off for the stride of the other leg. This practice strengthens the ankles and improves balance.
3. As you walk, extend your stride by an inch (2.5 cm) and maintain your rhythm.
4. After several minutes of practice, the pelvis may also move in opposition to the upper body.

Technique Progression 5:
Developing Stride Length

Stride length is the distance between the feet as you walk forward. It is also affected by limb length. Long legs generate more distance for your effort. A person who is 5 feet 2 inches (157 cm) takes two steps for every step taken by someone who is 6 feet 2 inches (188 cm). Likewise, tall people have a difficult time moving slowly enough to match the pace of a shorter person. This is perhaps the only limitation for Nordic walkers. The solution is to walk with friends of similar height, or to get into really good shape!

1. Use long arms, long legs, and cupping to enhance your stride length.
2. Draw your awareness to your leg speed and the distance between your feet.
3. Exaggerate stride length only as a drill in slow motion. Methodically step longer and slower, but do not bend your knee into a lunge. Your knees should remain relaxed, and your legs and arms should be long and coordinated.
4. Go up a gentle hill. Remain upright with good posture, avoiding loading your back and knees by bending at the waist. Going uphill develops stride length and works the muscles a little harder with every step.
5. On the descent, reduce your stride length and remain as upright as possible.

Complex Technique Progressions

It takes the average person about eight weeks to master concepts and skills for Nordic walking. Once the basics become automatic, other elements of skill come into play.

Technique Progression 6: Spine and Pelvic Rotation

As one of four recommended movements for a healthy back, spine rotation is a primary benefit of Nordic walking fitness. Notice how the shoulder follows the forward swing of the arm.

1. Stand upright without holding onto poles and try out a move of the classic dance, the twist. Although not exactly the same, the movement illustrates what opposing rotation feels like *(a)*.

2. Perform a style walk by intentionally placing one foot in front of the other. In this exercise, the upper torso initiates rotation and the pelvis then reacts by rotating in the opposite direction *(b)*.

3. Keep your chin level with the walking surface as you gaze ahead. Don't tip your shoulders laterally from side to side, but do exaggerate your saunter!

Technique Progression 7: Tip Engagement

This drill is only appropriate when the previous skills have been mastered, particularly long arms and awareness of spine rotation, which enable you to find the sweet spot on your tips and propel you forward with power and grace. At this point, you've had lots of practice time. If your arm swing is perfect, you have likely made contact with your tips, although every now and then you may still feel as if the tips are dragging or bouncing. This skill progression should take care of that! When the tip makes contact with the ground, that resistance creates an opposing movement of the torso and pelvis that is similar to how a fashion model walks down a runway. This practice dynamically stimulates all of your core muscles each time the tip makes contact. When performed properly, achieving tip contact is more of a sensation of contact, then an instant aeroplaning of the tip off the surface.

1. To engage the tip for fitness, deliberately increase grip pressure, starting at the forefinger and thumb *(a)*. Cup the bottom of the handle lightly to facilitate a smooth passive release. Too much grip pressure locks your upper body.

2. Receive the terrain with the contour of the rubber tip, rather than slapping it or planting the tip dramatically. There is no lifting, rather only an arm swing that effortlessly carries the tips *(b)*.

3. When you feel the tip make contact, delay the swing of your opposite leg until after you've intentionally pushed diagonally into the tip. You should feel the rotation of the spine and pelvis. Relish in the way it propels you forward!

4. Prepare yourself to step farther forward as propulsion begins.

Technique Progression 8: Handle Release

Low-impact Nordic walking techniques call for a passive handle release, in which the hand relaxes and opens to release the pole as it swings down by the thigh. This economy of motion equals efficiency of movement.

1. As you walk, pay attention to where your hands and arms start and end their movements.
2. After making tip contact, hold the tip to earth as long as you can while striding forward. Imagine your arm following the pole backward.
3. As your hand reaches your thigh, let the handle slip down the palm of your hand by relaxing your fingers.
4. Cup the handle as your arm swings the pole forward again.

Common Errors in Technique

The following list outlines primary biomechanical errors that can be eliminated or reduced by using proper skills:

- Overextending your stride length, or doing too much too soon, strains your lower back, groin, and knees. Take eight weeks to develop stride length.
- Gripping the handles tightly with bent elbows, lifting the pole tips off the surface, and planting them with force can strain the wrists, elbows, shoulders, neck, upper back, and lower back. While grip strength is important, relax your grip to target muscles of your back and core.
- Repeatedly moving your wrists out of neutral alignment at any point during the arm swing and especially upon tip placement to the surface strains the hands, wrists, elbows, and shoulders. The secret to decreasing impact is to keep your wrists neutral!
- Leaning forward to begin Nordic walking movements, or leading with the head, strains the lower back, upper back, and neck. This practice is counterproductive for back health because the average walker does not maintain enough speed or forward momentum to support the weight of the head. It also goes against the primary benefit of Nordic walking: better posture. Stand upright, keeping your chin level with the walking surface

and your head positioned over your pelvis. As you pick up speed, your body will naturally incline as it needs to.

- Be wary of bending your elbows at high speeds. When speed is increased, you need longer levers to effectively engage the tip and reduce the potential for injuries. Bent elbows are acceptable during slower, less intense, movements, since lower speeds decrease the chance of impact injuries. After eight weeks of consistent practice, you can play with enhancing speed.

You can further reduce the risk of injuries by becoming aware of the following errors in movements.

- *Lack of opposing-arm action.* Your natural arm swing should move in opposition with the legs.
- *Looking down.* This practice brings the weight of the head and shoulders forward, creating muscle imbalance in the rest of the body. Hold this heavy segment of the body efficiently over the pelvis. Cast your gaze ahead toward the horizon to promote good posture and muscle balance.
- *Waddling.* This error occurs when the upper body moves from side to side, causing the head and shoulder weight to move away from its orientation on top of the pelvis.
- *Failing to rotate the torso.* In this scenario, the upper body is stoic and frozen in appearance. Your arm swing should elicit a fluid rotation of the torso.
- *Excessively bent elbows.* Bending the elbows promotes a mentality of gripping, lifting, and planting instead of a long lever arm glide forward. Instead, extend your arms as they swing from the shoulder, keeping the elbows relaxed and slightly flexing only at the end of the swing.
- *Excessively flexed or extended wrists.* There are several reasons one excessively flexes or extends the wrists during striding. Most often it is the result of poles that are too long, forcing one's wrists to collapse toward the ground, or of one who is trying to mimic a picture or image of the classic cross-country handle "release". It may also come from the perception that the wrists should swing the pole tips forward as with trekking on narrow trails. Your wrists should stay in a neutral alignment. The arm swing should originate in the shoulders.
- *Death grip.* If your knuckles are white, you're gripping the poles too hard. Although grip strength is an important element of fitness, too much tenses the upper body and tightens the muscles, preventing efficient, fluid movement in the upper torso and core. Instead, relax your grip and cup the handles.
- *Painter's grip.* Holding the handle with the ends of your fingers (as if it were a paintbrush or a pencil) causes tremendous strain to the wrists,

elbows, and shoulders. Pressure on your little fingers is a sign that you have painter's grip. Your hands should be relaxed as you maintain full contact with the poles.

- *Thumbs up.* Don't point the thumb upward as you hold the handles. Instead, wrap your thumb comfortably around the handle and rest it on top of your forefinger.

- *Jazz hands.* Sometimes walkers actively open their hands and extend their fingers during the arm swing. Often they are trying to perform the classic release and get mixed up in terms of timing for the release movement, opening their hands in front of the body well before it's time to release the pole. Instead, relax your hands until they reach your hips, and then passively open them to allow the backward movement of the pole tip.

- *Overstriding.* This error, which is the second cause of Nordic walking injuries to the groin and lower back, usually happens when you increase speed and intensity too soon. Safely extend your stride over at least eight weeks.

- *Stepping to a full, flat foot.* This mistake results from lack of movement of the ankles and pelvis. Swing your legs forward with soft knees, make gentle heel contact, and roll your feet along the ground to the toes.

- *Bouncing tips.* When you initiate the forward arm swing with a bent elbow, your hand and arm may not move far enough forward to grip the ground with the contour of the rubber tip. It also happens when there is no grip strength at all. A little bit of grip strength as with cupping helps guide the poles to the sweet spot of the rbber tip, therefore eliminating the bounce. Use long levers to more effectively make contact with the ground. Sometimes the tips bounce with a long lever technique too. This is the sign of someone who simply has not had enough practice, usually because the arms do not swing far enough forward. Tip engagement takes practice to master.

CHAPTER 4

Stepping Up:
Variations for Cardio, Strength, and Power

Well-rehearsed skills and specific, detailed conditioning programs (parts II and III) diversify your Nordic walking training. Although part II focuses mainly on cardiorespiratory conditioning, you'll have other options to enhance your experience of full-body workouts. This chapter adds several components that take your training to the next level and enhance athletic ability and fitness level.

Complete conditioning for Nordic walking requires that you pay attention to your entire body, practicing upright fitness, safety during exercise, and consistent workouts. The best fitness programs progressively move you toward your desired outcome. Progressive training programs reinforce the skills of the activity for which you are training. It's good to be fit for a specific sport, but it's even better to cover those athletic bases in your daily workouts. More specifically, you can target individual components, such as agility or power. The result is that you are ready to improve your performance for just about any activity beyond Nordic walking.

Over time, your stride length increases due to the combination of long arm and leg movements and the resistance created by the pole's tips. Hills and speed intervals activate a lot more muscle through the tips. You must master that skill in order to accomplish the drills in this chapter because variations for complete conditioning include advanced cardio training, strength, power, agility, balance and coordination, and flexibility. You can accomplish all of these things with Nordic walking poles. Since the intrinsic nature of a Nordic walking experience is cardiorespiratory, you can also expect to improve the health of your heart at any level of intensity.

Aerobic fitness is the primary goal of cardiorespiratory exercise programs. The first step in your fitness program should be to build an aerobic base of long and slow distance training. When your heart and lung functions become more efficient, with greater stroke volume and oxygen utilization by the working muscles, you can increase the intensity of your training program to engage your anaerobic metabolism and advance your cardio proficiency. Advanced cardio training is the next logical step. The real intent of this book is to give you more ways to accomplish your fitness goals and to intensify Nordic walking workouts.

Advanced cardio training is most often performed in an interval format, which can be used to progressively increase intensity to improve cardio proficiency. When the energy demands are high, your body is only capable of sustaining that level of activity for seconds or minutes at a time. Training modalities that drive energy demands include plyometrics and sprints. You will quickly reach anaerobic threshold at the beginning of a drill, before oxygen supply equals oxygen demand, and when exercises increase the intensity. These shorter bursts of effort rely on stored in the muscles. Since muscles, tendons, and ligaments need time to adapt to anaerobic conditioning, interval training allows you to gradually increase the intensity of your workouts to reach your goals and prevent injury. Eventually, by systematically (with intervals) and repeatedly depleting glycogen in the muscles, you will increase your capacity for energy storage. At this point, activities that were once anaerobic become aerobic. Interval training maintains lean muscle mass and burns fat effectively.

The following training elements are components of sports proficiency, human performance, and Nordic walking fitness. All of the training programs in this book reference this chapter, which creatively represents exercises and drills to offer options for a balanced workout. How do you know when you are ready for training that is more advanced? Chapter 7 helps you choose the right path, but in the meantime, you will know you are ready when the routines of the past no longer satisfy you. If you are not getting results, it's time to walk with a stronger mission.

Advanced Cardio Training

As chapter 14 outlines, the benefits of cardiorespiratory conditioning are many. Other benefits include stress reduction, disease prevention, and weight loss. Advanced cardio training takes on a serious, yet meditative, quality.

Sometimes you have to meditate just to make it through the workout! At this point, you should have a plan to improve your ability as a fitness athlete. If you want to change your body composition, high-intensity training will do the job. Kicking your body's systems into a higher gear without hurting yourself requires experience, effort, and care. To start, measure your heart rate. Aside from being a good measurement of intensity, heart rate also indicates athletic improvement and adaptation to exercise. As your fitness level improves, your heart rate decreases with the same amount of effort as before.

If you are at an advanced level, you are typically already fit. You may also hope to master new and intense movements that involve multiple joints. Working out harder produces a stronger heart and more mitochondria, which deliver oxygen and nutrients through the capillaries to the working muscles. Capillary density makes this journey more efficient. Other benefits include decreased resting heart rate, increased oxygen consumption, enhanced blood flow to the muscles, and increased mobilization of fat stores for energy.

Heat, cold, and altitude play a role in the health of your body during and after movement. The probability of injuries increases because your muscles are pushed to their limits. Be wary of overloading your entire musculoskeletal system with accidental exuberance during advanced cardio training. You must warm up, cool down, and then stretch. However, for this kind of workout, it is most important to warm up by walking, gradually increasing the pace. At this level of conditioning it's prudent to also take a few minutes to perform some of the classic warm up exercises in chapter 7 to prime the joints for range of motion, and some dynamic flexibility drills in chapter 5.

Advanced Cardio Drills

These drills will inspire you to move faster on a couple of different levels. Although these elements are subjective, or specific to the athlete, all are important for athletic development. Leg speed is the rate at which your legs swing from the hip sockets. Consider the word *speed,* as in moving forward with great velocity. You develop your pace over time, combining leg speed and forward moving velocity. For some athletes, speed means breaking records, often by a fraction of a second. For most people, speed means moving faster than normal. Moving faster than normal is a realistic goal, but sprinting beyond capacity can be dangerous if you haven't worked up to it. Speed must be developed over time. In fact, some trainers slow their athletes down in order achieve faster speeds! This process fine-tunes mechanics before adding load (speed). You must mentally and physically master the skill components of the movement, one at a time, before building speed.

Turbo Walking

Objective

Increase speed for this full-body cardio exercise, which is sometimes performed in intervals. Your stride should be shorter, like the one used for fitness walking without poles.

Action

Decrease the range of movement of your arm swing (flexion and extension of the shoulders)*(a)*, which in turn decreases the range of your leg swing (flexion and extension of the hip)*(b)*, ultimately resulting in a quicker stride cadence that creates more strides per distance walked. This is a cross between the stride for power walking without poles and Nordic walking. The classic power walk involves short strides and bent elbows which pump back and forth to produce leg speed. Although the stride length is shorter, the legs remain long as the feet roll from heel to toes along the ground. This drill is most appropriate on flat terrain.

Variation

Use intervals to perform this technique in any aerobic or anaerobic capacity.

Benefits

Speed technique is a welcome break from long-stride endurance. Shortening the stride length engages the tip more quickly and with punch. Trainers with Nordic Walk Now call this technique Turbo Walking. Avid power walkers will love the similar cadence. If you are fit but new to Nordic walking, you can ease into it with this technique for a great experience.

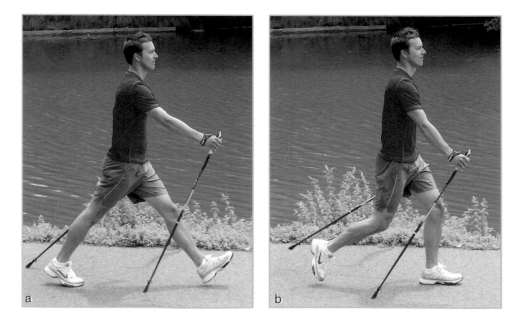

Injury Prevention

The rubber tips should make contact with the surface about a third more times than during a typical Nordic walking stride, which can increase the impact to the shoulders and back. Remember, you're not trying to plant the tip until it grows! Instead, make smooth and efficient contact with the entire surface of the tip to push through quickly.

Hill Training

Objective

Poles are great for cardio training on hills. Hills let you stay on the sweet spot of your tips longer. When going uphill, you take a little longer to accomplish your stride. Moving mass uphill simply takes more time, so it may feel as if you are moving uphill more slowly. With practice your speed, tempo, and pace will pick up. Striding uphill also adds load; it's more difficult because you are walking against the pull of downhill gravity.

Action

The longer you maintain tip pressure, the more resistance is transferred from the tips into your body. The longer resistance remains, more muscle is involved. Think of *moving through resistance*, rather than holding it. When going downhill, depending on the decline or pitch, you can use the poles tips either behind you or in front of you for support. Perform natural intervals while going up and down hills.

Variation

Any uphill terrain will do as long as it's not a narrow trail. Play with different pitches.

Benefits

You will gain strength and power in your lower body.

Injury Prevention

What goes up must come down. Momentum that is not managed properly can induce knee strain or worse. The combination of your body weight, stride

(continued)

Hill Training *(continued)*

length, speed of movement (which picks up on the downhill), and gravity will pull you downhill quickly. You must load your knees properly. Concentrate on connecting the feet fully to the earth, and flexing the knees and hips like an accordion to cushion the downhill impact. If the hill is steep, bring your pole tips in front of the body to cushion the pitch on the descent. Swing both poles forward, make contact, walk past the tips, and then swing forward again. If the hill is not as steep, use a slower version of speed technique. Push with the poles from behind the body, but take smaller strides.

Running

Objective

Cross-train for other sports with this version of an old favorite. Running with poles is a high-impact activity that is recommended only for people who are proficient at both running and Nordic walking.

Action

This style utilizes the short levers and upper- and lower-body mechanics traditionally used for running, although runners often experience a longer than usual stride length because of tip propulsion. Using the poles with bent elbows can injure the shoulder joint if you use improper technique. Maintain an angle of 90 to 100 degrees and hold your forearms parallel to the walking surface *(a)*. Experienced "super runners" play with even longer

pole heights to generate more resistance. Super runners are those who have a lot of running and training experience, who turn ordinary pole running into a graceful dance of athleticism, one that would send most people into their anaerobic threshold quickly. Move on and off the tips quickly. The tip becomes a fulcrum or pivot point that enhances forward propulsion and strength *(b)*.

Variation

Use your poles with intentional effort. Once you feel comfortable running with poles, push off harder to propel yourself forward with more velocity.

Benefits

For high-end athletic training, upper-body strength is used to generate power for bounding and jumping.

Injury Prevention

Because cadence and leg speed are quicker during running than during typical Nordic walking, the upper body works with shorter levers too. Impact is transferred to the wrists, elbows, then shoulders through the rubber tips. To make pole contact with less force, use the tip as a brief pivot point as you move forward. Get on and off of it quickly!

Strength Training

Strength is the prerequisite for intense power training. Furthermore, it produces positive adaptations that improve balance, agility, and more. Coordinating simultaneous movements requires full-body effort to support the demands of repetitive motion and endurance. Core stabilization requires muscular endurance of the torso, since Nordic walking reintroduces rotation of the spine. If performed safely, a balanced strength program results in muscle balance and back health. Lack of appropriate strength may result in injuries, especially for walkers who change their stride length overnight.

During striding, you gain strength by generating forward momentum in two ways. First, upper-body muscles can be loaded with resistance through the tips. Second, increased tip contact creates more stimulus for greater strength. The slower your pace, the fewer times you will make contact. But, you can play with that concept. The longer you stay on the tips, the longer your muscles are activated!

This chapter provides exercises that build strength by targeting various places in the body. Some, like walking lunges, can be performed either on the fly or in intervals. Like traditional strength-training drills, some are stationary and others require concentration of movement, sets, and repetitions.

The following strength and power exercises allow you to gradually increase strength and muscle endurance. Beginning with the lower body and progressing to the upper body, these exercises represent a full-body strength workout that is specific to Nordic walking. These exercises and drills are referenced in part II.

Exercises and tasks do not need to look like Nordic walking to be effective. However, most of the following exercises are performed on your feet, using the poles, the natural environment, or intensity of movement to add resistance. Most strength exercises can be performed in repetition. If an exercise calls for work on one side, be sure to do the same amount of repetitions on the other side as well. Select one of the following three strength categories (see chapter 7 for further discussion of these categories):

- *Skill development workouts.* Perform one set twice weekly at about 20 minutes per workout: 8 to 12 reps of 8 to 10 exercises.
- *Fitness proficiency workouts.* Perform two sets twice weekly at about 30 minutes per workout: 10 to 12 reps of 8 to 10 exercises.
- *Competition workouts.* Perform two or three sets twice weekly at about 45 minutes per workout: 10 to 15 reps of 8 to 10 exercises.

The method for upper-body stability while performing the exercises is referenced several times in the following sections. To perform the V pattern, open your arms in front to a position wider than your hips, holding the pole tips comfortably in front but open to the sides like a "V" to provide a strong base of support.

Lower-Body Strength Drills

The following exercises provide strength conditioning for the hips, pelvis, upper and lower legs, ankles, and feet. Since most of these exercises are closed chain, which means either your legs or arms are in contact with a fixed surface, other muscle groups are at work as well, including those in the upper body and the core. These lower-body exercises facilitate solid stride mechanics and overall strength, which is the key to using Nordic walking for fitness. Because fitness requires practice, create a stable connection between lower-body muscles and the pull of gravity to become proficient.

Foot and Ankle Rolls

Objective

Conditioning the lower legs is essential for executing smooth striding movements. This exercise targets the muscles surrounding the ankles. To involve the muscles of the ankles, feet, and toes, roll your foot along the ground, from the heel all the way to the tips of your toes.

Action

Use poles in a V pattern for stability. Stand with your feet in a walking position and your toes pointed forward. Gently roll up on the balls of your feet *(a)*, and then back down on your heels, raising the toes slightly *(b)*. Perform this exercise without thrusting your hips or straightening your knees. Keep your center of mass slightly lower than usual, moving primarily from your lower legs and ankles.

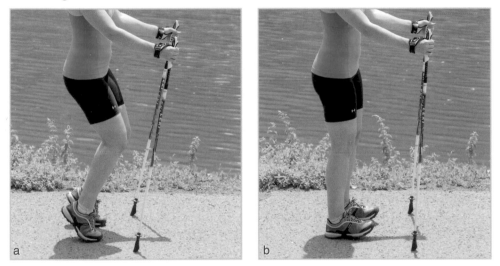

Variations

- Balance on the balls of your feet for five seconds. This variation conditions you for equilibrium.
- Lift one pole tip away from the surface to challenge your balance. This variation challenges stability and strength. Pay attention to ankle movement for balance recovery.

Benefits

Movement through the ankles facilitates leg speed and balance. This is also great ski/snowboard training.

Injury Prevention

Your movements should come from the lower legs, ankles, and feet. The knees should remain relaxed and not overextended.

Old-Fashioned Squats

Objective

Squats are a prerequisite for power training, which is presented later in this chapter. Think of this old-fashioned version as the warm-up for activities with a higher impact. All of the muscles of the core, torso, pelvis, and lower body are involved.

Action

Use poles in a V pattern for stability. Place them about 10 inches (25 cm) to the sides and in front of your toes. Open your stance to a position that is slightly wider than your hips. Point your toes to the positions of 10 and 2 on a clock. Lengthen your arms to move the poles outward for support. Hinge your hips back to feel balance. Bend your knees to lower your center of mass. Press back up through the soles of the feet to an upright position.

Variations

- Move twice as fast, obviously with less range of motion. This practice mimics sports like cycling or Alpine skiing, and is a great low-impact power drill.
- Hold the poles in front of you like cat whiskers at an angle, keeping wrists in neutral. As your body lowers, raise both arms upward. Lower your arms as your body extends back to standing position.

Benefits

The squat is one of only a few primal movements that is necessary throughout life.

Injury Prevention

Don't load your toes as you lower or rise. Allowing your knees to jut forward in front of your toes causes knee strain.

Lunges

Objective

Lunges are another primal movement that primarily strengthen the quadriceps and hamstrings and stabilize the femur (thigh) during forward striding. They also train your body for better balance and stability through movement.

Action

Use poles in a V pattern for stability. Extend one leg behind your body to create a distance about three times longer than your normal stance. Step forward with the front leg, aligning the knee over the heel of the foot

to bear the majority of your weight. Raise and lower your pelvis (center of mass), maintaining knee alignment (the knee should not protrude beyond the toe).

Variations

- Alternate legs during lunges.
- Perform continuous and dynamic walking lunges. Using the poles for stability, lunge forward with one leg, and then immediately follow with the other.
- Perform dynamic, low-impact, multidirectional lunges. Lunge as if stepping toward positions on a clock face. Step between 1 o'clock and center, then 3 o'clock and center, etc.

Benefits

Because you are working larger muscles, you are burning more calories.

Injury Prevention

Take the same precautions as for squats; don't load those knees. You should not extend your knee past your toes. If you are lunging correctly, you should be able to see the top part of your foot in your low position. If you cannot see your foot, simply extend your lunge by an inch or two (2-5 cm).

Single-Side Squats

Objective

This exercise conditions the legs separately. Although the primary muscles are the quadriceps and hamstrings, concentrate on your abductors and adductors, which balance your weight and support your core effort.

Action

Using poles in a V pattern, stand on one foot, slightly flexing the ankle and knee on that side. Extend the other leg in front of you and pull the knee up to the height of your hip. Focus on your abdominals and hip flexors as you do this. As you pull the knee up, drop your pelvis 2 to 5 inches (5-10 cm) toward the ground, depending on your strength. Maintain upright posture, flexing your hip, knee, and ankle on the support side. This exercise trains you for agility because the secret to moving quickly from one foot to the other si a solid sense of equilibrium on one side independent of the other, and practice in that element.

Variations

- During the upward phase of the exercise, concentrate on fully extending your ankles to raise your heels. On the downward phase, visualize your joints moving like an accordion as your hips, knees, and ankle compress which is also protocol for impact reduction during plyometrics.
- Lift one or both pole tips off the ground to challenge balance.

Benefits

This exercise is the prerequisite for squat thrusts (see page 69).

Injury Prevention

Maintain balance by softly gazing toward the horizon. Don't stare at a single object intently. Rather, take in the large landscape.

Multidirectional Leg Lifts

Objective

This exercise conditions the muscles surrounding the thighs for dynamic balance, muscle endurance, and range of motion.

Action

Perform this exercise by standing upright and holding poles in a V position. Balance on the support leg and foot. Lift the other leg out to the side, then back to center, then behind you, then back to center, and then to the front. Lift only to heights that allow you to maintain upright, natural posture. When you feel your head, shoulders, or pelvis moving off center, you have reached your strength limit.

Variations

- Perform the exercise without putting down your foot.
- Hold each position for three seconds.

Benefits

The powerful hip flexors and extensors connect to the core on the front and back of the hip to sustain strength and alignment even with intense forward momentum.

Injury Prevention

Maintain upright posture. Don't lift the leg too high. If your upper body tips in the opposite direction, you are not strong enough to support this level of effort. This exercise does not include momentum—it is not a leg *swing*. It's a lift using purely your own strength.

Backside Strength

Objective

This strength exercise somewhat resembles the classic dead lift. Both versions enliven the hamstrings and lower back with flexibility and strength.

Action

Stand with your feet hip's width apart, hold both poles in front of you in a position that is horizontal to the surface, and relax your arms and place them on the front of your thighs *(a)*. As you exhale, extend your tailbone behind you to move your upper body into a forward bend *(b)*. Keep the poles and hands on the front of your legs as you slide down until you reach your limit *(c)*. Gently hold the poles against your body for support, and then roll back up. As you start moving back up, stand firmly on the soles of both feet, stabilizing the weight of your upper body with your hamstrings. Your head should roll up last. Soften your knees as you stand back up with excellent posture.

Variations

- When your pelvis is fully flexed downward, waft from side to side. This variation enhances flexibility in the lower back.
- Lay bean bags over both ends of the poles or in the center to add resistance.

Benefits

This exercise enhances flexibility in the hamstrings and lower back.

Injury Prevention

If you have a history of lower-back pain, skip this exercise. It may produce more strain.

Old-Fashioned Step-Ups With Bench

Objective

This drill develops balance, *slow-moving* strength and general lower-body conditioning.

Action

Stand facing an 8- to12-inch (20- to 30-cm) platform, low wall, or bench. Hold the poles in a V pattern, placing both tips on the ground next to your feet. Slowly step on top of the platform with the right foot, followed by the left. Push off the ground with your poles. As you rise, you may choose to place the tips on top of the bench. Use the poles for stability as you move the right foot back to the ground first, followed by the left foot. Perform this drill slowly.

Benefits

While traditional lunges enhance stride length, these create more power in a vertical motion. As you rise up, pay attention to weight transfer especially that of your upper lead leg. Strength combined with effort to stabilize the knee protects your body as training becomes more intense.

Variation

Set your poles down for a while. Rely solely on your lower body and core strength.

Injury Prevention

Two kinds of injuries are typical with this type of exercise. First, the height of the platform may bother your knees or lower back. Start with a lower platform and work your way up in height. If you can't step to the top without breaking forward at the waist, your platform is probably too high. You should be able to maintain upright posture throughout. Also, take care that you don't fall off the platform. If you have injured your knees in the past, this drill might not be appropriate.

Core Strength Drills

The following exercises provide strength conditioning for the abdominal, back, and gluteal muscles to facilitate trunk stability, balance, postural endurance, and spine rotation. These muscles hold the joints in proper orientation and hold the spine in alignment with pelvic stability.

Standing Rotations

Objective

The objective is to isolate your midsection with a twisting move-ment. This action also causes spine rotation, which is an impor-tant element of Nordic walking fitness and technique.

Action

Assume a stance slightly wider than your hips. Place poles over your shoulders and hold them behind your neck. Maintaining upright posture, relax your knees without bending excessively. Rotate your torso to the right, and then to the left. Move slowly and with control. Stay light on your feet.

Variation

Soften the knees even more for this variation, which involves a full-body rotation. Perform the rotation as previously described, but as soon as you reach 80 percent of your full range of motion, shift your weight to the balls of your feet, and then continue rotating with the pelvis, completing a full-body pivot around your toes. Your knees and hips will flex.

Benefits

This is a great warm-up movement. The variation improves dynamic balance.

Injury Prevention

Move with control, being careful not to overrotate.

Woodchoppers

Objective

Use the poles as subtle weights as you move through several different ranges of motion. Woodchoppers improve oppositional strength for plyometric drills like bounding by safely enhancing your range of motion with resistance.

Action

Stand with your feet hip's width apart. Use one or two poles to perform a diagonal, downward-chopping motion. Hold the middle of the poles and then turn them diagonally toward your body. With relaxed knees, draw both hands up to the right *(a),* and then press them down to the left *(b).* Repeat for the recommended number of repetitions, and on both sides.

Variation

Reverse the movement. Start by holding the pole on the ground on the left side, and then pull up diagonally to the top side.

Benefits

This exercise enhances strength and flexibility for Nordic walking muscles by including leg, core, and upper-body resistance.

Injury Prevention

Shift your weight during rotation. For example, as you chop down toward the left side, your right heel raises, allowing a slight pivot of the left support leg.

Resistance Rotation With Partner

Objective

Typically, you do this type of training with a pulley apparatus in a health club. The object of this fun exercise is to feel your partner's resistance as you move slowly through a rotational range of motion. Because this exercise can be intense, you may choose to omit some reps at first.

Action

Share one set of poles with your partner. Partner A stands in a lunge position about one foot in front of B. A places both poles on her shoulders, similar to Standing Rotations on page 52. B's role is to place both hands on the poles to the inside or outside of A's. As A begins a subtle rotation, B's job is to hold the poles in place and provide resistance, as if not allowing A to rotate. Be sure to lunge to both sides, repeating the drill, then switch roles.

Benefits

Use this exercise to cross-train for sports like golf or baseball, which rely on strength and resiliency of the trunk.

Injury Prevention

Partner B should be careful not to apply too much pressure to A's poles. The workout is intense enough. To keep things safe, move with A while providing subtle resistance.

Back Extensions

Objective

Sometimes it's necessary to stop, drop, and be strong! This exercise improves posture and pelvic strength.

Action

Lie on your belly. Position one or two poles under your chin, holding your hands shoulder's width apart. Lift your head an inch (3 cm) off the surface, keeping your forehead parallel with the ground. Extend both arms in front of you, and then bring them back in, relaxing your forehead to the ground.

Variations

- Raise both your legs and arms to a level height and hold them for a few seconds before relaxing back down.
- Try to shift your upper and lower bodies laterally.

Benefits

This exercise is excellent for postural strength and pelvic stabilization. Spine extension is also one of the four healthy back movements.

Injury Prevention

This exercise does not require a lot of range of motion because movement comes from the extension of the spine. Overextension of the spine strains the lower back, especially if you also actively lift your head off the ground. To avoid this, visualize an eyeball on the back of your neck. Keep the eye open as you lift!

Opposing Arm and Leg Raises

Objective

Training the back side of the body for bilateral strength complements the rotational efforts of Nordic walkers and decreases the potential for injury.

Action

Get down on the ground on all fours, placing your knees and hands directly under your hips and shoulders. Have a friend place a pole horizontally on your back. Extend your right arm out in front, eliminating one of the four balance points. Next, extend your left leg backward, removing another balance point. You are now resting on your left hand and right knee. Try to keep the pole from falling off as you move. Repeat by extending the opposite arm and leg.

Variations

- Try this drill without a partner or without a pole.
- Try holding onto another pole with the extended arm. Grasp the handle and point the pole away, or grasp it in the middle and lift horizontally off the surface.

Benefits

Balancing your own weight is a healthy type of strength training. Using the pole also throws stabilization into the mix. Stabilization requires use of the core muscles.

Injury Prevention

Do not lift the leg and arm higher than the position of your body. Lifting too high is counterproductive and takes away from a balanced strength approach of this exercise. It's easy to lift the leg higher than the arm. Instead, even out your effort and position your limbs and hips level with the ground.

Front Press With Partner

Objective

This full-body exercise requires upper-body strength as you move while trying to hold off your partner.

Action

Face your partner, holding the poles between you with an overhand grip. Lean forward into the resistance of your partner, and move with each other to react to the resistance. This drill involves trust! This exercise is timed.

Variation

Lie on your backs, holding one pole between you and your partner with both sets of feet! This exercise becomes a leg press with knees bent. The object is that you both work to keep the pole from falling to the ground and to react to the pressing resistance of your partner's leg.

Benefits

This playful favorite requires concentration and full-body strength.

Injury Prevention

Leaning forward takes a lot of trust. Select a partner who is of similar height or weight.

Upper-Body Strength Drills

The following exercises provide strength conditioning for your chest, upper and lower back, shoulders, forearms, and core, which is often involved by default.

Obviously, a well-tuned upper body can help you maintain good posture in endurance situations that are more extreme. These muscles hold the back and spine in alignment over the pelvis. Upper-body strength also balances out muscle effort during striding. Of course, your goal is to use the pole tips to spread the physical effort out so the upper and lower bodies work in unison.

Underhand Rows

Objective
Because Nordic walking involves pushing through the tips, this exercise produces resistance in the opposite direction by pulling to balance out upper-body strength.

Action
Hook both poles around a small, stable tree or post and grab each end with an underhand grip. Stand facing the post or tree and move into a quarter squat *(a)*. Your poles should be just below your chest. Pull your body toward the post *(b),* and then return to starting point.

Variation
Switch to an overhand grip and move the poles up higher on the post to a position that is level with your chest. This makes resistance higher in your upper back.

Benefits
This is great cross-training for water sports like rowing and kayaking.

Injury Prevention

When moving into a quarter squat, do not lower your hips below the knees. Keep the hips elevated about an inch (3 cm) or more above the knees to avoid overloading the knees.

Classic Push-Ups With a Twist

Objective

This classic upper-body exercise is as old as the hills and is always effective! Perform it without poles to increase overall upper-body strength.

Action

Leave your poles behind and find a car bumper or park bench. Place your hands on a bench at a position

slightly wider than shoulder's width. Extend your feet back, moving your body to a position that is diagonal to the ground. Keep your lower spine neutral and use core muscles to stabilize your body as you move your chest toward the bench. Push back up, but do not completely straighten your arms. Keep your elbows relaxed and soft throughout the entire range of motion.

Variations

- Try Teeter Poles. Holding both poles horizontally in front of you, place them across the end of the bench. Perform the push-up while holding the poles, creating a lateral, teetering feeling.

- Standing upright, hold both poles horizontal to the ground with an overhand grip. Your hands should be slightly wider than your shoulders. Maintaining a slight bend in your elbows, press toward the center of the poles as if you could fold them. This practice creates isometric resistance.

Benefits

This exercise generates equilibrium in the upper body, which stimulates proprioceptors in the wrists, elbows, and shoulders.

Injury Prevention

Even if you train classically with free weights, pushing your own weight is the foundation of other modes of strength training. If performing the teeter-totter, be very careful to properly balance the poles over the top of the bench to be sure they are evenly balanced to avoid tipping too far over.

Triceps Press

Objective

The objective of this drill is to strengthen the triceps and rear deltoids to facilitate precise tip placement and load with appropriate pressure.

Action

Place one or both poles behind your body and hold horizontal to the ground. Assume an upright stance with feet placed hip width apart or a moderate, split-lunge stance. Grasp each side with an underhand grip, holding your hands slightly wider than your shoulders. Extend both

arms away from your body, and then release them slowly toward your backside while your partner applies slight resistance.

Variations

- In an upright stance, rest the poles in front of you at the hip crease. Place the palms of your hands against the poles to the sides of your hips. Arms should be slightly wider that your shoulders. Press into the pole, and then release from an isometric contraction.

- Stand in front of a park bench. Rest one pole across your lap, and place the palms of your hands against your thighs as if you were going to sit. Move your pelvis away from the bench just an inch (3 cm). Raise and lower your hips, keeping them level with the ground to avoid dropping the pole.

Benefits

This exercise tones the underarms nicely, as well as the muscles of the shoulders, chest, and back.

Injury Prevention

Only lift the poles behind you in a range of motion that is comfortable. If you lift too far, you'll break at the waist to accommodate the movement. Instead, maintain upright posture.

Double Poling

Objective

Repetition of movement builds an efficient and automatic stride. This drill is an author favorite because it very effectively strengthens the back while you are on the move. Use both tips simultaneously for resistance and powerful forward propulsion.

Action

Use both poles at the same time to push off and thrust forward. Take two strides between each push-off.

Variation

Use only one pole at a time to push off. Tuck the other one under the corresponding arm.

Benefits

This exercise strengthens large back muscles and the arms, specifically the lats and triceps.

Injury Prevention

Be careful not to overuse your shoulders. For single side poling, you should do no more than eight repetitions on each side of your body per interval. Be sure to train both sides evenly when doing one-sided drills.

Multidirectional Arm Raises

Objective

This dynamic exercise takes the arms and shoulders through varied movements and ranges of motion. It also uses the poles to add a surprising amount of resistance. Optimal function of the shoulders during Nordic walking relies on proper alignment. Multidirectional results in the use of multiple muscles. This exercise thoroughly conditions all the muscles that surround and support the shoulders, which activate the muscles of the chest and back.

(continued)

Multidirectional Arm Raises   *(continued)*

Action

Hold one pole in each hand at its center. Place your hands at your sides, holding your palms toward your thighs. The poles should point in front of you and behind you. Stand with neutral, upright posture, relaxing your elbows and wrists. Lift both poles laterally up to the height of your shoulders *(a)*, and then lower them back down. Rotate your wrists toward the front of your thighs, and then lift both arms toward the front, crossing the poles *(b)*. Finally, lower them back down.

Variations

- Hold the poles horizontal to the ground in front of your body. Lift both arms, first in front of your body, and then out diagonally as if you were spreading your wings. Move your hands up and out, and then back down to the front of your thighs

- Place poles in a V pattern. Simply press downward into the surface to create resistance in the upper body. Change tip placement to move them closer. Notice how resistance moves to different muscles!

Benefits

Working the arms and shoulders in this manner is perfect for recovering from injury.

Injury Prevention

Momentum is a good thing only if you can maintain perfect posture throughout all the movements. This means you are strong enough to move a little faster. Remember, prioritize form before speed!

Power Training

Simply defined, power is strength plus speed. The results of power training determine which sprinter leaves the blocks first, which skier pulls out a win by a hundredth of a second, or which Nordic walker picks up the pace for the final stretch of a marathon. With muscle gains that are functional as well as aesthetic, power training enhances the body's ability to jump, run, and lift. Powerful athletes are less susceptible to injury and excessive fatigue associated with long-term performance. They can have the aerobic capacity to sustain pace and the anaerobic power to surge ahead of the pack.

Many sports require anaerobic power. Examples include slam-dunking a basketball, using sprints to score a goal in soccer, and racing up a steep dirt trail with a mountain bike. Nordic walking shares this explosive (quick and powerful) muscle quality.

Power training is characterized by repeated loading and unloading of the involved joints in rapid succession. Training includes high-impact drills like sprinting and plyometrics, and low-impact options like continuous dynamic lunges.

Injury Prevention for Power Training

Many training drills require that you take both feet off the ground simultaneously, during which speed combined with the impact of landing can damage your body. Extreme athletes often say "You don't get hurt in the air; it's the landing that gets you!" Careless landings can abnormally tax the joints, spine, and muscles, producing strain or injuries that are even worse.

Traditionally, people associate impact with exercises that involve pounding on a hard surface, such as running. Other types of subtle impact take place during Nordic walking. Extending your stride length too soon negatively affects the pelvis and lower back. Repetitively pounding or planting the pole tips directly affects the health of your shoulder joints. You can eliminate these mistakes with proper technique.

At first, you should approach these power drills with a low-impact mindset. This means practicing them outside of your workouts. Proficiency, rather than airtime, is your primary objective. After a thorough warm-up, practice techniques for proper takeoff and landing. As you practice these drills, don't go for speed. Slow down and think through the movements. The following section outlines tips for preventing injury, as well as some low-impact modifications.

Safe Techniques for Taking Off and Landing

The following high-impact drills describe common techniques for taking off and landing safely. The objective is to facilitate power on the takeoff and resiliant cushioning on the landings. Some of the drills require a one-foot lead, while others dictate that both feet come off the ground at the same time. Some require the use of one pole; others use two poles. Both cases involve hang time, in which both feet are off the ground. The interesting element that differentiates the Nordic walking version of these drills from the traditional execution is that the poles create a brief point of contact as both feet leave the ground. These drills can also serve as a stepping stone to athletic training that might not have been possible before. These techniques are not difficult to learn but they do require practice for proper form. Regardless of the drill, keep the following guidelines in mind:

- *Takeoff.* You usually use tip resistance to aid either forward or upward propulsion. These drills require strong abdominals, hip flexors, and calves to raise the knees and legs. Some drills require that both arms move forward at once, but most use typical opposition. Remember to keep your wrists in neutral, regardless of arm height, for a safe push-off and release. To propel forward with one leg, push off with the opposite pole and extend your leg forward. For stationary jumps and forward leaps with two feet, extend your arms extended down toward your sides, and then thrust them up or out for momentum.

- *Landing.* Ensure a soft landing by cushioning the ankles, knees, and hips in succession, as when an accordion compresses. For stationary jumps, concentrate on your toes, ankles, knees, and hips. For drills with forward motion, concentrate on your heels, ankles, knees, and hips. Keep your chin level with the walking surface to avoid breaking at the waist. Extend at the hips, knees, and then ankles when jumping either up or forward.

Impact Modifications

If you find the impact of the power drills presented here to be too much, the following considerations will help you reduce impact. You may simply be making errors in technique. You can also modify exercises to reduce the intensity. As you perform the drills more and more, your body will adapt, allowing you to do the unmodified versions. Don't push yourself to do these new drills and skill sets too soon. You already know it takes time and a lot of practice to learn skills properly. Once you are proficient, you'll be able to do the interval segments as recommended. The sky is the limit, literally!

- If you find jumping with two feet too difficult, opt for drills that lead with one foot. Many people find skipping the easiest to learn and perform.
- Don't go up in the air until you feel comfortable. For example, when learning bounding, you can move forward in slow motion to decrease the amount of airtime.
- Stationary jumps are perfect for practicing low-impact modifications because your feet do not move far from the ground to get a killer lower-body workout.
- Constantly check to see if your joints are in alignment. The wrists are the worst culprit! Remember that your body functions best when your joints move in a neutral position, regardless of the fitness activity or sport.

- Look forward, focusing your eyes ahead instead of down at the ground. This practice appropriately situates the weight of the head and shoulders on top of your spine.
- Start at a pace that is slow, stay low, and just go!

Power Training Drills

Perform power drills in timed intervals rather than in repetitions. This way, you can work with a buddy to perform the same drills at your own tempo and pace. You must march to your own beat when it comes to high-impact activity. Never train at a friend's pace and tempo unless it's a match to yours exactly or you're using it as a drill. With practice, you will find a safe pace and tempo. If a workout calls for one minute of bounding, don't feel as if you must complete the entire minute. Instead, perform three or four bounds to help your body adapt to this kind of overload. Adaptation is also a personal process. On average, you should practice two or three times per week for four to six weeks before adding power training to your workouts. These practices do not take long, but they help you work safely and execute the drills properly.

Stationary Jumps

Objective

Use your feet, legs, and arms simultaneously to jump straight up and land in the same spot. Begin with a low-impact version, perhaps even staying on the ground for the first few repetitions. Over a period of weeks, you'll gradually jump higher.

Action

Use the poles in a V pattern for stability. Move into a half squat by softening the hips, knees, and ankles. Press down on the tips to generate upward body movement and to prepare the lower body to jump. The tips may come off the ground. Land by absorbing the ground like an accordion, relax the ankles and knees and flex at the hips to absorb the impact. Keep your chin level with the surface.

Variation

Do the drill in place with one leg at a time. This variation is a prerequisite for skipping.

(continued)

Stationary Jumps *(continued)*

Benefits

This drill prepares you for forward leaps by accomplishing lengthening muscular contraction, which reduces impact and over time strengthens the tissues surrounding the knees.

Injury Prevention

If your knees are healthy, this type of activity will likely make them stronger. However, if you have knee problems, this type of activity may produce more stress than benefit. Start slowly and stay low to the ground.

Tuck Jumps

Objective

This intense lower-body drill is driven purely by power.

Action

Hold the poles under your arms as if you were a ski racer. Poles should be parallel to the ground and pointing behind. Poles are not actively used in this drill. Assume a modified tuck position by supporting your upper body with your hands on thighs. Look ahead, not down. Using your arms for upward momentum, extend straight up in the air through the lower body. As your feet leave the ground, retract your knees up toward the abdomen. Land as described for the stationary jump. Eventually you will be able to perform a full tuck.

Benefits

If you have a healthy back, and you like impact, the load on the lower body will make you feel stronger than ever. Rock climbers use this more like an agility drill for resiliency and quickness.

Injury Prevention

This drill requires a tremendous amount of core strength to protect your back during both phases of the jump.

Forward Bounding

Objective

Use long levers combined with pole propulsion to create power. The extended stride length and unweighted air time let you reach the pole even farther in front of your body to make tip contact.

Action

Bounding *(a-b)* is performed by moving one leg forward at a time. Long arms and legs move in opposition just as for Nordic striding. Delay moving your leg forward until you feel solid tip contact from the opposite side, then push back on the tip and bound forward with the opposite leg. The tip pressure is your signal to bound forward.

Variations

- Use two poles to push off instead of one, swinging both arms forward between bounds.
- Move forward diagonally with one or two poles.

Benefits

Bounding is a staple drill of track-and-field athletes. It prepares the body for sports like hurdling and ice hockey. With poles, it's the ultimate full-body training drill. There is nothing like that feeling of fully engaging your lats!

Injury Prevention

It's easy to become overly zealous in your ambition to perform this drill properly. Start slowly, and then gradually increase distance and airtime. The more you use your upper body to propel forward, the more success you'll have in the lower body.

Forward Leaps

Objective

This drill involves all the skills of the stationary jump, but adds forward movement, allowing you to generate momentum.

Action

Use your arms and poles to aid forward momentum. Extend both arms and poles forward. When you have made tip contact, push back against the poles and leap with both legs, pulling the knees upward then extending the legs forward *(a-c)*. Cushion the landing by first making contact with the heels, and then flexing the ankles, relaxing the knees, and flexing the hips.

Variation

Use the pole tips as fulcrums. Leap forward, then backward.

Benefits

This drill is a staple of power conditioning and is plain, old fun. Champion bull riders use this drill to train for impact management.

Injury Prevention

It's one thing to absorb impact while jumping from a stationary position, and another to cushion impact while moving forward. In this drill, be sure to land from heel to toes.

Squat Thrusts

Objective

Aim to train one leg with more intensity than you do for the other. This drill takes single-side strength to a new level of dynamic balance and proficiency.

Action

Stand to the side of a curb, low bench, or some other kind of platform. Hold the poles in a V pattern, with one tip on the platform and the other tip on the ground *(a)*.

(continued)

Squat Thrusts *(continued)*

Perform this drill from a stationary position; do not move forward. With one foot on the ground and the other on the platform staggered about four inches (10 cm) ahead of the other foot, press into the pole tips and extend upward for momentum, and then extend your lower body *(b)*. Land as you would for a stationary jump.

Variation

To maintain a low-impact experience, rise up as if intending to leave the surface, but stay on the ground. Instead, extend more from the ankles to move as high as you can without jumping.

Benefits

As long as you train both sides of the body, isolated limb training on uneven surfaces is actually good for you. The changed range of motion stimulates different muscles.

Injury Prevention

An uneven surface always presents a challenge for balance recovery. Be sure that your top foot lands appropriately on top of the curb, and your other foot lands on the ground rolling from the toes and balls of the feet to reduce impact. Landing half on and half off on the ground of the surface could lead to sprained ankles.

Power Skips

Objective

This is perhaps the most fun of all the high-impact drills. Bringing you back to your childhood, the power skip combines skipping action with forward movement and airtime. Skipping is a full-body effort that creates power in the core, hip flexors, and thighs, which contract to reduce impact.

Action

Begin by hopping with the left foot, while simultaneously lifting the right knee. The left arm and pole move forward in opposition to the right knee. Make contact with the left pole to trigger the process again. The tips are a powerful addition to this exercise that work the body bilaterally.

Variations

- Try speed skipping, literally skipping faster. Adding this element of agility decreases distance and airtime. Perform two speed skips for every power skip.
- Rotate the legs open as the knee comes up to target the deep rotator muscles of the hip joints.

Benefits

Because of the opposition of the upper and lower body, this drill improves core and spine rotation. It is also great for sports that require power and quick movement, such as basketball and tennis.

Injury Prevention

Since this is a relatively easy drill to learn, you'll go farther and higher than in some of the other drills. Land proficiently to avoid twisted ankles.

CHAPTER 5

Changing Pace:
Variations for Balance, Coordination, Agility, and Flexibility

Now that you've experienced advanced cardiorespiratory techniques and strength and power training, think of balance, agility, coordination, and flexibility as the icing on the Nordic walking cake. These ingredients complete your fitness package, helping you avoid silly falls, acquire efficient speed technique, and complete difficult exercises. Add these elements to your workout routine to effectively condition the nervous system for all-around proficiency.

This chapter provides exercises and drills, many of which are incorporated into the six four-week programs in part II. The great thing about this type of training is that it can be done almost anywhere. It's easy to find a place to perform a balance or agility drill. Furthermore, these exercises are within the capabilities of most people. Most people enjoy the spice and spontaneity of these playful exercises, which can be applied to contexts other than Nordic walking. If someone you know really needs to get outside and work out, invite them to play with you! Even if they never complete a single stride of Nordic walking, they can use the poles to improve their general fitness.

This chapter outlines drills in terms of progressive intensity, listing them in order from easiest to hardest. Intensity also depends on the amount of repetitions completed.

Balance and Coordination

All physical activity requires some degree of balance or equilibrium, an internal blueprint of the dynamic reactions, involuntary sensations, and impulses that keep us standing upright. Your body's balance centers, the eyes, ears, hands, and feet, work together to sense imbalances and to correct posture. To understand how the body works to balance efficiently, think about how it feels to transfer weight from one foot to the other while walking. As you extend one leg forward, feel your center of mass (located in the pelvis) move over that leg and foot to momentarily restore balance. Balance awareness is a simple concept that can drastically improve anyone's fitness level and health.

Balance and coordination allow your body to work all components of fitness and movement, especially skills and cardiorespiratory function, with precision and efficiency. They are fundamental elements of functional human movement, health, fitness, skill development, and athleticism. Balance and coordination involve a complimentary relationship of movements enabled by efficient reactions that flow smoothly and rhythmically from one skill process to the next, allowing you to perform tasks unconsciously. Examples include your breath, heartbeat, and natural walking stride. The same principles apply to Nordic walking.

Skilled Nordic walkers move efficiently, making small but constant adjustments that complement balance to safely manage body movements. As they stride, several simultaneous movements occur as the body, which strives naturally for rhythm, smoothly coordinates movements. Nordic walkers should difficult to slow down enough to recognize these small, constant transitions. Their execution of dynamic balance, or balance in motion, is a result of hard work and practice. Specific balance training enhances technique and enjoyment, conserves energy, and reduces risk of injury.

Balance and Coordination Drills

Although these exercises are not physically demanding, they require slow and calculated concentration to develop body awareness and muscle memory. During agility and power drills, your own reactions to the movements may challenge your balance. Stationary balance drills, which are performed from an upright standing position, are appropriate for warm-ups and cool-downs. Dynamic balance training combines all of the athletic qualities in this chapter including balance awareness and coordination.

These drills facilitate smoother transitions as constantly changing postures force you to trust your innate sense of balance. Poles are used functionally for stability, but they also enhance the effectiveness of the drills. The drills that are performed while moving are the most fun. Although they challenge coordination, you'll find that your balancing efforts are automatic. Many of the tasks are timed in intervals. Others can be toned down and used for your cool-down.

Single-Side Balance Awareness

Objective

This drill marks the first step toward acquiring skills for balance and coordination. Remember you must balance and stabilize the legs during every stride in Nordic walking, not to mention coordinating opposing arms and legs. This simple task can change the athletic disposition of most uncoordinated people.

Action

This drill is performed from a stationary position. Use poles in the V pattern for stability. First, distribute your weight evenly between both feet. Shift your pelvis slightly to the right until all your weight has shifted over to the right foot. Stand in this position for a few seconds to acclimate the right side of your body before lifting the other foot. Lift your left foot an inch (2 cm) off the surface and drag the toes a few inches to the back. Both feet should still be in

contact with the ground. After a few more seconds, lift the left foot a couple of inches off the ground. Practice this for one minute on each side.

Variations

- Play with your vision by focusing in different directions, and then into the horizon. Where are you looking when your balance feels best? Most likely, you're gazing off into the horizon with your neck held in neutral and your chin held level with the surface. This orientation protects you from back strain.
- Lift one pole off the surface. Add a strength component by raising and lowering your center of mass as in a single-side squat.

Benefits

This task is appropriate for people who have artificial joints or prosthetics for the lower extremity. With practice, they can see great improvements in proprioception and balance. This task is also a prerequisite for power drills like squat thrusts and bounding.

Injury Prevention

This task is pretty simple because the poles provide stability. This is an appropriate drill for most people. It can also be highly effective for those athletes who have neurological issues or conditions such as Parkinson's disease and cerebral palsy. In this case we recommend it under the care of a physical therapist or physician. If you lose your balance, simply touch the free foot to the surface for a moment, then resume. Use the poles to help you finish out the length of the interval.

Partner Mirroring

Objective

Follow a partner's movements while balancing on one foot. The task is to duplicate or mirror your partner with enough coordination to maintain balance. At first, try this from a stationary position. This timed task should be performed for 30 seconds on each side.

Action

Face your partner about 4 feet (1 m) away. Each of you should balance on your right foot. Partner A leads performing a variety of challenging movements, and partner B tries to follow them. After one minute, partner B leads.

Variations

- Use forward, lateral, backward, and circular movements.
- Try it with direction—the classic "follow the leader".

Benefits

This task forces you to move ways you may not consider typical as you march to someone else's beat. This type of training inspires new learning in the muscles and joints because it is impossible to plan out your reactions.

Injury Prevention

Be sure you have enough space to move your limbs and poles in a variety of planes and directions. If you lose your balance, place the free foot on the ground momentarily, and then resume.

Controlled Jousting

Objective

As in the previous drill, you will balance on one foot and react to your partner. However, this task requires that you each hold on to the ends of one pole, as in a tug-of-war. Basically, you play to win, working to throw your partner off balance. You can also lose by putting your foot on the ground to recover your balance. No mercy with this one! It's all in fun!

Action

Using one pole between two of you, stand five or six feet (1-2 m) away and face your partner. Each person holds one end of the pole and balances on one foot. Begin to joust, trying to force your partner off balance by pushing and pulling.

Variation

You can fake each other out by playing with resistance. For example, create a consistent rhythm of push and pull, and then add a surprise power push.

Benefits

Of all the exercises, drills, and tasks, this is the authors' favorite because it is the most fun to perform.

Injury Prevention

Jousting is fun, but it also poses the most risks because of jabbing poles, adjustables that are not properly adjusted, or accidental falls. It is possible to joust someone hard enough to cause a fall. Simply put your foot down on the ground if you feel you are about to lose your balance. Jousting is most effective when partners are of a similar height and strength.

Partner Choo-Choo Train

Objective

This skill-driven drill improves Nordic walking technique, specifically long-lever movements from the shoulders. It trains the shoulders to be more adaptable under load and for range of motion.

Action

Use a set of two poles for two people. Partner B stands behind A. Each partner grabs the ends of both poles. To get started,

try arm movements without walking. Then, both begin a slow stride—B follows A in cadence and rhythm. As you start walking in good timing with each other, B controls the pace and timing of arm movement.

Variation

You can do this alone as a warm-up drill by holding both poles by their centers. Work to keep them level with the walking surface. If one end of the pole comes up, relax your grip. Let the poles float over the surface.

Benefits

By now you know how important it is to move the legs and arms freely to create and sustain rhythm. This drill loosens up the arms, shoulders, and upper back, which also assists spine rotation. Arm movement is the key to torso movement. This drill emphasizes the importance of an extended arm during Nordic walking.

Injury Prevention

Because the person in the back dictates the rate of arm movement, very little pole guidance is likely enough. It doesn't take much effort to overdo the assistance and generate too much arm movement for the person in front. When you are in back, check in with your partner periodically to be sure the pace is appropriate. The hands of the partner in front should never swing higher than the navel. If the poles have straps, either clip out of the handles or don't put them on to begin with.

Synchronized Walking

Objective

This advanced coordination drill enhances rhythmic transition from stride to stride. It relies on two (or more) people. One follows the cadence and rhythm of the other.

Action

Partner A is the lead and sets the pace and stride length. Partner B mimics identical movements in the same timing. To get in sync with A, B stands slightly to the side, behind A. As A walks, B follows A's arm movements. The objective is to make tip contact and propel forward at the same time and rate as your partner.

Variations

- Lead with different stride lengths.
- When leading, take five strides to the left, then five to the right. Partner B's task is to maintain cadence with direction change.
- Add more walkers and follow the leader.

Benefits

Another author favorite, this fun drill inspires efficiency of movement. Partners each get to play two roles. As the leader, partner A must concentrate on timing and technique. Partner B reaps most of the benefits through reacting to A's movement cues. Quicker reaction times help you prevent accidents, improve dynamic balance, and win races.

Injury Prevention

It's possible to walk too close to the lead person. When you are following, stagger yourself to the right or left of the leader to watch the lead arm. Stand far enough back to feel like you have your own space and to avoid tripping on your partner's poles.

Walking Backward

Objective

This drill is intended for the cool-down period. Some researchers maintain that the body needs to be trained for a variety of directions and loads.

Action

Hold one pole in each hand by its center. Poles should remain horizontal and floating above the walking surface. As you slowly walk backward, keep your chin level with the surface. Allow the arms and legs to move in opposition.

Benefits

Placing your body in a somewhat unfamiliar situation aids balance and stability. It forces you to think about what your feet are feeling as they touch the surface.

Injury Prevention

Walk in an area that is free of traffic and dangerous deviations to terrain, like potholes!

Agility

Generally cardiorespiratory by nature, agility involves fast footwork, such as sudden starts, stops, and changes in direction, and requires muscular control and balance. You must carry out tactical decisions in a precise and timely manner. Use Nordic walking poles to enhance quickness and maneuverability. Perhaps one of the best qualities of agility training is that most people can become successful with relative ease. Agility drills are especially cool because they are not as intense as power drills. They are easier to learn but present a different kind of challenge.

Agility Drills

The following drills are timed in intervals to let you move at your own pace and concentrate on the movements themselves, rather than being concerned about the number of reps. Although some of these drills do possess power attributes, more emphasis is placed on precision, maneuverability, and speed with agility. These drills will enhance your overall versatility as an athlete.

Step-Ups on a Curb

Objective

This is the introductory agility drill. Although it is stationary, you must move your feet quickly. As you perform intervals, be sure to change your lead leg for the second half. This drill is primarily cardiorespiratory, but it also improves dynamic balance, focusing effort on the feet and ankles for quick and precise foot movements.

Action

If you've ever seen or taken a step aerobics class, this is similar. Position the poles in a V pattern, with the tips on top of a step or curb. Slowly step the right foot up so that its full length is on the step or curb (not just the ball of the foot). Next, bring the left foot up, then take the right foot down, followed by the left foot. Gradually increase your speed until you feel like you are jogging in place.

Variations

- Step onto the curb in a V pattern, placing the feet wide during the ascent, and then back to a neutral stance on the ground.
- Run it! This is when it's appropriate to spring off the balls of your feet.
- Try it without poles.

Benefits

This is a classic drill for indoor exercise. If you have done step aerobics before, feel free to play with other footwork patterns.

Injury Prevention

Wear proper footwear. Sprained ankles are the most common injury from agility exercises. Rapidly changing directions, even when traveling a short distance, can upset your body's ability to accommodate directional load. Select footwear with lateral stability to prevent tripping.

Single-Side Agility

Objective

Single-side ability is the key to human locomotion. These drills require dynamic balance because they train one side at a time. Combine single-side balance with speedy squat thrusts for the ultimate agility training! Your objective is to move quickly without the use of poles for stability.

Action

Place both poles horizontally on the ground in front of you. They should be about 18 inches (50 cm) apart. First practice this drill with both feet. Then, stand on one leg and hop forward and backward over each pole. Maintain balance, only touching your free toe to the ground if you fear you will fall.

Variation

Get some sidewalk chalk and draw the ultimate agility course in the form of a hopscotch grid. First, leap forward with both feet. Next, try one foot at a time.

Benefits

These drills enhance proficiency for future power training that is more advanced. If you've conditioned your body to remember what jumping and landing feel like, you will easily be able to add airtime and forward movement.

Injury Prevention

If you lack strength in the core, gluteal, and thigh muscles, hopping on one foot can strain the lower back. Wear foot beds or athletic inserts for additional support and try them with both feet.

Crossover Walk

Objective

This drill uses Nordic walking techniques. It loosens up the upper back and inspires core strength for greater spine rotation.

Action

Nordic walk at a fitness pace, crossing one foot in front of the other as you go. As the tips make contact, the pelvis reacts by rotating in the opposite direction. Your shoulders move in opposition to the pelvis. Try running to pick up your cross over pace.

Benefits

If you desire to try out for *America's Next Top Model,* this is the right drill for you. Models are athletes in stilettos, right?

Injury Prevention

Although this is one of the easier drills, walk with care if you have back or hip problems. If you choose to run, be careful with this one. Some coordinated athletes have "gone over the handle bars" tripping themselves with their own poles.

Flexibility

Flexibility equips us with the mobility to move freely in various directions. Increasing that range enhances kinesthetic awareness, which is partly derived from the proprioceptive input of your nerves, muscles, and bones. This book heavily emphasizes posture because the use of poles greatly enhances the potential for muscle balance and recruitment. Furthermore, poor posture promotes overdevelopment, underdevelopment, or overuse of muscles, which can train proprioceptors (nerve endings in the muscles and tendons that respond to stimuli regarding the position and movement of the body) to send faulty information through the nervous system. This prevents the nerves from supporting the muscles through the desired actions, especially those requiring endurance. Dynamic flexibility exercises use controlled movements to activate the joints, which then stimulate those lively nerve endings for quicker, more accurate transmission of instructions to the involved muscles.

To develop a proficient stride, Nordic walkers must learn to work with the effects of gravity and speed. Usually, you perform well within the limits of your musculature. Still, it only takes one unplanned fall to make you appreciate your body's resilient ability to bounce back. In short, increasing your flexibility will increase the range of safe motion and effort. When you are strong and speedy enough to simultaneously respond to cardiorespiratory demands and the forces that upset balance, flexibility will give you the elastic mobility to reestablish functional posture, regardless of intensity.

Dynamic Flexibility Drills

Exercises for dynamic flexibility typically involve a combination of standing upright and moving in some direction along with the exercise. Unlike static stretching, when you hold a position to lengthen the muscles, the hold time for dynamic flexibility is shorter and is based on your own strength. These types of exercises have recently become popular with fitness facilities and athletic trainers because they let athletes keep moving. Therefore, you can easily combine these drills with cardio training.

Perform these exercises first from a stationary stance, then attempt to incorporate forward movement. Regardless of the exercise, lift your legs only as high as you can without the help of momentum. For example, you may be able to kick your leg up to a certain height in a forward leg lift. However, if you do not have the physical strength to slowly lift your leg to that height and then hold it without struggling to maintain your posture, you have no business kicking that high.

These upright exercises are performed in repetitions. Like any other weight-bearing exercise, pay attention to posture before load. The lumbar spine, ankles, head, and neck should remain in neutral alignment. When the joints are forced out of a neutral alignment, the body functions abnormally, leaving you at risk for injury either now or in the future. Neutral alignment enhances joint function, helping them do their job much more efficiently. Since these exercises can generate momentum, stay grounded in your effort by maintaining efficient posture.

Leg Swings

Objective

This exercise prepares your body for additional flexibility drills and enhances leg movement from the hip joints. This is the only exercise that does not allow you to move forward while performing it.

Action

Use the poles in an open V pattern for stability. Balance on one foot, and then slowly swing the other leg back and forth *(a-b)*. Control the swing. Start with a limited range of motion. After 10 repetitions, begin to extend your range.

Variations

- Add lateral leg swings. For example, swing the right leg out to the side away from your body, back at a slight diagonal in front of and across your support leg. Plant the poles a little farther apart to give your leg enough space to swing through.
- Mirror your leg movement with the opposite arm and pole.

Benefits

You can perform this drill either during the workout or as part of the warm-up.

Injury Prevention

Too much swing creates momentum that may put stress on the lower back and tight hip flexors.

Backside Kickers

Objective

This exercise focuses on your lower body muscles, specifically the hamstrings and the gluteus maximus. We don't really recommend kicking yourself in the backside; instead, these movements can take hip extension with knee flexion to healthy ranges of motion. Be sure to warm up first. Begin this drill in a stationary position, and then add forward movement after a few reps.

Action

Use poles in a V pattern for stability. Balance on one foot and flex the knee of the other leg so that your heel moves toward your backside, and then put that foot down. Alternate sides and repeat. With practice, you'll feel your foot approaching your backside and the extension in the front of your hip.

Variation

Try it while walking forward or running forward. Stride length will be shorter.

Benefits

Strong hamstrings protect the integrity of the knee and the surrounding connective tissues.

Injury Prevention

When the heel comes up too high, the back may arch accidentally. If you can't perform this exercise without arching your lower back, slow your movement down because you need to strengthen your backside and increase flexibility in the front, exactly what this exercise promotes! Instead, maintain neutral posture the entire time as your guide for how high to lift.

Knee Lifts

Objective

The opposite of backside kickers, this exercise promotes flexibility for the back side of the body and strength for the front muscles, hip flexors, and core.

Action

Use the poles in a V pattern for this stationary drill. Balance on one foot. Flex the knee of the other leg, bringing the thigh and knee toward the navel. Alternate sides and repeat.

Variation

Try this drill while walking or running forward.

Benefits

This drill is great for core training because strengthening the hip flexors also works the abdominal muscles.

Injury Prevention

If your core is weaker than other areas, you may break at the waist as your knee comes up. Maintain efficient and neutral upright posture throughout the movements.

Forward Leg Lifts

Objective

This drill takes knee lifts to another level of intensity because it is performed with a long, extended leg. The poles are also used differently to create resistance in the upper body.

Action

Use the poles in a V pattern for stability. Balance on one foot, and then extend the other leg out in front as if to kick something. Perform this movement with control. Repeat for both sides.

Variations

- Try this drill while walking forward.
- Add the upper body. Hold the poles with more downward pressure to use your back muscles. As the leg comes up, press down. Repeat on both sides.

Benefits

This drill engages the upper body for a full-body exercise.

Injury Prevention

When you extend the levers, your risk for back injury goes up. Remember, less momentum equals more strength.

Continuous and Dynamic Walking Lunges

Objective

This exercise takes an old favorite forward. Adding the forward component engages twice as many muscles.

Action

Using the poles in a V pattern, practice some stationary lunges. Next, start moving forward, lunging with one leg, and then the other. Use the poles for a dual push off, then bring them forward, draw the lead leg through, and so on.

Variations

- As you walk, lunge diagonally to target the rotators that support the pelvis.
- Slightly decrease your stride length and range of motion to pick up your pace, and then use ankle strength to spring up in between strides.

Benefits

Dynamic walking lunges train the lower legs for balance recovery because ankle movement is an inherent requirement of the exercise.

Injury Prevention

It's even easier to overload your knees in this drill than in stationary lunges! Load the heels and mid-foot instead, rolling from the heel to the toes and off.

Stationary Flexibility Drills

Stationary stretching develops elasticity in the muscles and range of motion within the joints. Lack of stretching makes muscles short, tight, and unresponsive. When sudden tension forcefully extends those tight muscles, it creates microscopic tears in the tissue, resulting in soreness or pain. You might experience this type of injury if you change your stride length overnight or by doing too much too soon. You must warm up to prepare your body for the range of motion of subsequent workouts. Perform these stretches at the end of your workout from an upright position, holding them for 15 to 30 seconds.

Stretch for Obliques and Back

Objective

This drill stretches the obliques, the quadratus lumborum, and the erector spinae.

Action

Take the poles in both hands and extend them overhead, holding the arms farther than shoulder's width apart. Open your stance a little wider than hip's width apart. Push your right hip to the right side, and reach your right hand straight up and slightly to the left, allowing the poles to pass over the shoulders. Repeat the action for the other side.

Variation

Put the poles down and find a tree branch or use the monkey bars at a park to hang from, allowing you to stretch your upper body.

Benefits

This is one of the four movements for a healthy back. If you do this drill every day, you'll notice more strength and resiliency through your core.

Injury Prevention

Your goal is to lengthen both sides of the body instead of shortening one and lengthening the other.

Stretch for Lower Back and Hamstrings

Objective

This drill stretches the extensors of the lower back and the hamstrings.

Action

This drill is similar to the exercise for backside strength, but the stretch should be held longer. With each exhale, allow the head and neck to relax downward completely. You'll feel the hamstrings and lower back release, allowing your head to lower even further. After a few breaths, come back up to a standing position by softening the knees, pushing up through the feet, and rounding the spine upward. The head will roll up last.

Variation

Neck relaxation is key to relaxing the rest of your body. Try sitting in a chair and taking a breath. As you exhale, round forward and relax your head down.

Benefits

If you have a healthy back, this stretch relieves back tightness. It is good for people who must sit for long periods at work.

Injury Prevention

Don't do this stretch if you have back injuries. The weight of your head and shoulders will place more strain on an unhealthy back.

Stretch for Chest

Objective

This drill stretches the pectoralis major, the anterior deltoid, and the biceps.

Action

Bring one or two poles behind you and hold them horizontal to the ground. Grasp it with both hands, open your chest, and gently lift the pole behind you.

Variation

Try the drill without poles. Stand in a doorway, place your hands on its sides, and walk a couple of steps forward so that your arms are stretched behind you. Lean forward to feel the stretch in your chest.

Benefits

Humans spend too much time doing activities that draw the head weight unhealthily forward, such as typing, driving, and eating. This drill is important for postural balance and elicits safe spine extension—another of the four healthy back movements.

Injury Prevention

If you've ever injured your shoulder, you know how sensitive this joint is. Stay in tune with your body to know when stretching becomes straining.

Stretch for Back and Shoulders

Objective

This drill stretches the latissimus dorsi, the rhomboids, and the deltoids.

Action

Perform this stretch without poles. Move your left hand across the body to a position in front of the right shoulder and place it on a fence or bar that is a little higher than chest height. Similarly, reach across to the left with your right hand and grasp the bar. Soften your knees and shift your weight over the left foot, extending your left arm as your body crosses over. Next, shift to the right side, lengthening the right arm.

Variation

Perform the exercise with a partner. Face your partner with a wide stance and stand about 4 feet (1 m) away from each other. Each of you should cross your arms so that your right hand holds his right and your left hand holds his left. This stretch involves trust! Move into a half squat and lean your mass back. Extend the arms to feel the stretch along both sides of your back.

Benefits

Whenever the lats are active, other muscles automatically become active too, regardless of the modality of training. If you only have time for one stretch, this is an excellent choice.

Injury Prevention

Both of these options involve trust on some level, since you're leaning backward with your entire mass. Be careful not to drop your mass too low during this stretch. Keep your pelvis level or slightly higher than your knees. If doing the variation, don't drop your partner!

Stretch for Front of Thigh

Objective

This drill stretches the quadriceps and the hip flexors.

Action

Hold one or both poles with your right hand for stability. Reach back and grasp your left foot. Keep the knee aligned under the hip, stand tall, and tuck your pelvis under to feel a stretch in your hip flexors and quadriceps. Repeat this action on the other side.

Variation

Lie facedown on the floor. Grab the right foot and gently pull it toward your backside. As you exhale, take the stretch higher into your hip flexors.

Benefits

Since the quadriceps are one of the largest muscle groups in your body, they need more stretching (along with the hamstrings) to keep your back healthy. Stretching the hip flexors is the added benefit.

Injury Prevention

Hyperextension of the spine during this stretch is the result of a weak core. Regardless of your orientation to the pull of gravity (standing or lying down), keep your lower back in neutral.

Stretch for Back of Thigh

Objective

This drill stretches the hamstrings, the gluteus maximus, and the extensors of the lower back.

Action

Hold a pole in each hand for stability. Extend your left heel and soften the knee of the right support leg. Push your tailbone backward to lever the left leg. Flex the foot to balance on the heel and stretch the back of your leg. Repeat for the other side.

Variation

Place your heel and leg atop a platform or bench for more range of motion.

Benefits

Knee and back health are a reliable benefit of stretching the hamstrings.

Injury Prevention

This stretch is done by levering the hips back. Avoid breaking forward at the waist, which minimizes the benefit to the hamstring by engaging the back instead.

Stretch for Outer Thigh

Objective

This drill stretches the abductors, the tensor fasciae, and the piriformis.

Action

Use the poles in a V pattern for upright stability. Cross the lower right leg over the left thigh. Do a quarter squat on that side. Repeat for the other side.

Variation

Lie down on your back. Pull your right knee toward your chest and cross the lower right leg over the left thigh. Place one pole through (in between) your legs so that it is horizontal to your body. Grab both ends of the pole and pull your right thigh forward to increase the stretch. Repeat for the other side.

Benefits

When these muscles are flexible, the spine can easily rotate while striding.

Injury Prevention

This stretch requires balance and back strength. Don't break at the waist.

Stretch for Inner Thigh

Objective

This drill stretches the adductors and the internal rotators.

Action

Use the poles in a V pattern for stability. Separate the feet to a distance farther than hip's width apart. Bend the right knee and shift your weight to the right to stretch the left inner thigh. Flex the hip to enhance the stretch, feeling it deep inside at the insertion of the adductors to the pelvis. Move over to the left to stretch the right side.

Variation

Stand laterally to a low platform. Place the left (inner) foot on the platform and soften the right knee to add more range of motion.

Benefits

Stretching the inner thighs creates flexibility in the lower back and strength in the abdominal muscles.

Injury Prevention

Often people overstretch these muscles, effectively pulling the groin muscles. Be sure to thoroughly warm these muscles up before stretching.

Stretch for Back of Arms

Objective

This drill stretches the triceps, the rear deltoids, and the latissimus dorsi.

Action

Hold a pole vertically behind your back. Extend your right hand overhead to grasp the top of the pole. Grasp the lower end of the pole with the left hand. Slowly, move the right and left hands closer together. Without disrupting your posture, pull down with the left hand. Switch sides.

Variation

Do this one without poles. Place your right hand behind your head to touch the left shoulder. Use the left hand to apply pressure to the right elbow, stretching the back of your arms.

Benefits

This drill stretches more than the back of your arms. You'll feel it all the way down to your obliques.

Injury Prevention

The shoulder is the most active joint in this stretch. Be careful not to overdo it. Stretching is effective until it feels forced. Listen to your body.

Stretch for Back of Lower Leg

Objective

This stretch is for the muscles of the calves, including the peroneus longus and brevis, the gastrocnemius, the soleus, and the tibialis posterior.

Action

Place both poles in the right hand, holding both tips about one inch (3 cm) in front of the right foot. Balance on the left side with a soft knee. Squat on the left side and place your entire right foot on the poles, in the lengthwise section above the tips. As you exhale, stand taller and pull the handles of the poles toward your body. Repeat on the other side.

Variation

Use the poles in a V pattern for stability. Step on top of a curb or stair with your entire left foot. Step up with right foot, but only place the ball of the foot on the curb or stair (the other half is hanging off). On an exhale, balance on your left foot and drop your right heel to stretch the back of your lower leg.

Benefits

During a stride, as the heel makes contact with the walking surface, the calves automatically lengthen and stretch. As you roll through to the toes, the calf muscles shorten. These lower leg muscles need to stay supple and flexible to accommodate leg movements and longer stride lengths.

Injury Prevention

If you are thinking your poles will break, although manufacturers do not advocate trying to break them nor do they replace poles intentionally broken, you are likely incorrect. Your poles (adjustable poles included) are made to withstand pressure. If you decide to do the curb stretch, do not hyperextend your knee. Keep it soft while stretching the calves.

Stretch for Front of Lower Leg

Objective

This drill stretches the muscles of the front shins, including the tibialis anterior, the extensor digitorum, and the hallucis longus.

Action

Using the poles in a V pattern for stability, cross your left leg and foot over the right, and wrap the left foot around the lower right leg. Your left toe should touch the ground on the other side of your right foot. Balance on the right side and soften that knee, gently pressing the right knee into the left calf to stretch the front of the lower left leg. Repeat on the other side

Variation

Place the entirety of your right foot on a curb or low stair. Wrap your left leg in front of and around the right leg. Hook your left toe on the curb.

Benefits

Wrapping your limbs around each other requires coordination and balance.

Injury Prevention

These stretches require a good sense of balance. Use the poles for stability.

Stepping Out:
Adapting to Different Terrain

Environmental awareness is as important for your workout as skills are for learning efficient Nordic walking. If you are comfortable in your walking environment, you will progress faster. You alone are responsible for preventing injury during Nordic walking. Safety extends beyond Nordic walking techniques. One of the greatest factors that affect your experience is terrain selection. Beginners should choose even surfaces for mastering skills and seasoned walkers can choose hills to enhance their technical experience.

Although the outdoors provides an optimal environment for Nordic walkers, many research studies about the use of poles have taken place on a treadmill. While this may seem like an oxymoron, there is more to Nordic walking than exercising outside! Mall walking and *Polates* (a hybrid of Pilates and Nordic walking) have become popular forms of indoor group exercise in certain parts of the U.S.

Gear

As previously discussed, you can prepare for weather and ground surfaces with the proper gear. Dress in lightweight, breathable layers that wick away moisture. When the weather is hot, you will sweat! Hydration systems are a must. Several convenient ways to carry water exist, including CamelBaks and Aquaclips. Both attach to your body. A CamelBak is more of an investment, but Aquaclips only cost a buck fifty and work well if you don't want to carry anything on your back. Other options include specially designed belts and packs for carrying bottled water around your waist. A lightweight backpack is also useful on longer walks for carrying a hat, sunscreen, and a light energy snack.

When temperatures reach freezing, wear layers of lightweight, warm, and breathable clothing, as well as a knit hat, neck gator (a neck sock which slips over your head to cover your neck) and gloves. Most pole straps can adapt to comfortably fit a lightweight pair of gloves.

Until recently, Nordic walkers have had difficulty walking in snowy and icy conditions. Now, products like Kahtoola Microspikes can help you maintain a fitness pace in the winter. This new product, which easily fits over your shoes, has miniature spikes that are strategically placed to enhance balance while walking on the ice. Spikes reduce the chance of slipping on ice to almost zero. Walking on a freshly plowed winter road with the absolute ease of your typical summer pace is an amazing feeling! Just take the rubber tips off your poles, and you're ready to go.

You may also enjoy using snowshoes for Nordic walking in deeper snow. Keep in mind that it is impossible to maintain a brisk pace as you lift the poles and snowshoes out of the snow. Hold the poles in front of the body for stability in varying snow depths. Because snowshoes are more cumbersome than regular walking shoes, plan on a leisurely pace. This process still provides a heavy workout. Lifting snowshoes in and out of the snow repeatedly is like using a StairMaster.

Terrain Selection

Most people prefer the good old outdoors and an open road! Ideally, your terrain should include a paved or dirt road that is free of traffic. Since your poles require a path that is 4 feet (1.2 m) wide, single-track hiking trails are not ideal. Neighborhoods and parks are perfect for Nordic walking. However, if walking on narrow sidewalks with others, be wary of accidentally intertwining your poles. Beach boardwalks, bike paths, and dirt roads are popular terrain choices because they are wide enough to accommodate more than one walker at a good clip, and have little interference from crosswinds.

Since Nordic walking poles are very lightweight, walking in heavy winds or cross winds can be particularly dangerous and should be avoided. Winds can easily push the poles sideways or out of your control. When walking in any kind of heavy wind, pay attention to its direction to avoid tripping. Maintain two body lengths between yourself and other people or objects.

If you live in the U.S., contact the Bureau of Land Management to learn about dirt roads near you. These dirt roads are often free of crowds and traffic. If your dog can follow you without a leash, bring him along! Of course, this circumstance is more appropriate for rural areas.

Adjusting Technique for Different Terrain

Hills are obvious outdoor elements that can be used to enhance fitness and training. Both uphill and downhill techniques can be modified to enhance contact of the tips to the surface. When going uphill or downhill, some Nordic walkers prefer to shorten adjustable poles by a few centimeters to expedite tip contact.

Going Uphill

When climbing uphill, remember to keep your chin level with the walking surface and start with your head and shoulders over the pelvis. This will allow your body to adapt to forward movement appropriately, causing a forward tilt that is a natural reaction to your speed and climb, instead of intentionally leaning forward first. The poles help you maintain upright posture without bending forward at the waist (6.1*a*), which strains your back. The distribution of effort over four points of contact instead of just two also relieves pressure on the knees, which are no longer excessively bent or *loaded*. One instructor reports that her fitness program, called the Kamikaze Uphill, is accessible to most people because poles reduce strain on the knees and back.

Take eight strides to get into your groove, and then increase your stride by 1 inch (2 cm). It is more difficult to feel your leg swinging from the hip when going up a steep hill. The incline makes you feel as if your knees are bending more than usual. Focus on relaxing the heel of the front foot, rolling through the

Figure 6.1   Poles allow you to stay balanced with efficient posture, even when walking uphill. The faster one walks, the more pronounced the forward movement of the torso is.

foot as you step. This practice helps the knees cushion the effort. If you have healthy knees, this practice will strengthen them. If your knees require loving care, tread gently through the heels, maintaining a consistent shorter stride. To enhance tip contact, allow the opposing arm to swing even farther toward the front (6.1*b*). The contoured terrain of the ascent guides the tips toward their sweet spot.

Going Downhill

For walking downhill, use some of the techniques of mountain trekking. Begin with a shorter stride than you typically use for Nordic walking to counteract the momentum you acquire when moving downhill. You must contend with two pulls of gravity. One pulls your weight straight down into the earth. The other pulls from the direction in which you are traveling. Use the warm-up period to prep for downhill shorter striding. In accordance with the laws of nature, there is no need to intentionally change your stride length. Do what feels natural and best for your body.

Excessively planting or striking your heel as the first point of contact with the ground and pull of gravity can take its toll on your body. If the physiology of the foot and heel is disrupted, your knees will be less able to cushion your muscles as you step downhill. When the knees don't function properly, effort centers on the lower back. It's a vicious cycle of inefficiency. Step gently, feeling the length of your foot from heel to toe with every stride.

With experience, you can work on agility, balance, and coordination as you go down hills. Once you are accustomed to downhill striding, play with tempo

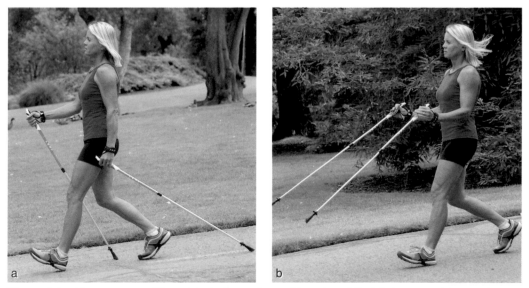

Figure 6.2   Here are two different techniques for walking downhill: *(a)* shorter strides and shorter arm swings, and *(b)* double poling, a technique borrowed from trekking, which works well on steeper declines to cushion downhill effort.

by walking at a clip similar to fitness walking. Concentrate on rolling your feet over the surface with every stride. This increase in speed can challenge your balance. You'll always be able to recover if you know what is going on under your feet. You could also try decreasing your speed to move in slow motion. This practice works the lower body.

When going downhill, you can use either the typical diagonal push-off (6.2*a*) or a trekking technique (6.2*b*) to cushion the impact. Simultaneously swing both poles to the front, plant them, walk two or three strides, and then swing the poles again. You could also swing one pole through, walk three strides, and then swing the other one forward.

Nordic Walking Versus Trekking

This book makes several references to trekking, the cousin of Nordic walking. This simple analogy illustrates the difference between the two sports. Nordic walking is to trekking what road biking is to mountain biking. Although many people mistake one activity for the other, the equipment is actually very different. Using trekking poles for Nordic walking is kind of like using a putter to golf a nine-hole course!

Can the two types of poles be used interchangeably for Nordic walking and trekking? While both techniques provide similar health benefits, it's important to note that most people who use trekking poles are not working toward a killer cardio workout. Moreover, after practicing Nordic walking on a wider path, you will quickly become frustrated on narrow trails, where the tips of Nordic poles usually get stuck in shrubs. Trekking poles can be used for Nordic walking. However, the heavier trekking poles have an angled handle and strap that accommodates movement of the wrist and hand as you swing the pole tips forward.

The weight and feel of the poles are different also. Nordic walking poles are extremely sleek and lightweight, with handles and straps that allow the hands to relax in order to target the larger, wrapping muscles of the back. Nordic walkers hold the tips behind the body, keeping their arms long and making tip contact at a diagonal angle.

Use Nordic Walking Poles for Fitness

Nordic walking and road biking are steady-state aerobic activities. Both improve cardiorespiratory health as you propel forward. Nordic walking poles are streamlined for speed on wide, paved areas, such as bike paths and streets. Dirt roads are ideal. As in cross-country skiing, the poles equally distribute your body's physical effort. You can burn more calories than fitness walking the old-fashioned way. Most important, the use of poles facilitates excellent posture, which is essential for maintaining a healthy back.

Nordic walking poles have two sets of tips. One set is rubber and is used on streets and sidewalks. The other set is spiky and resembles the tips found on the poles of Nordic walking's close cousin, trekking. Although they are mechanically different, both sports enhance stability and back health, and activate the muscles of the upper body. Nordic walking might not have evolved without the rich history of trekking.

Use Trekking Poles for Hiking

Trekking and mountain biking are done in rugged mountainous areas, on narrow trails, and in undulating terrain. Athletes maneuver through twists, turns, drop-offs, and varying terrain at a moment's notice. Ground surfaces include dirt, gravel, talus, pumice, sand, grass, and anything that isn't man-made! Therefore, the equipment is built to facilitate balance and stability for maximum safety on the trail.

Trekking poles do not come with rubber tips and are made exclusively for hiking and negotiating narrow mountain trails. They are heavier and are designed with swing weight, which brings the tips forward for stability and balance when negotiating varied terrain and crossing streams. In fact, the techniques used in trekking are the opposite of those used for Nordic walking because the tips of Nordic walking poles push the body forward from behind.

Commonalities

Regardless of their application, using poles of any kind automatically stimulates your spine and all the muscles around it. This is true even if your technique is inefficient! The resistance you feel through the tips as you walk is called *tip-to-grip biofeedback*. Even if you don't understand what's happening, the dynamic relationship between the tips and your grip activates key postural muscles of the core and upper body. The more skilled you are, the greater the benefit to the nervous system and the rest of your body.

Guidelines for Outdoor Safety

Pay attention to the weather by dressing for it and staying hydrated. You should also consider the fact that Nordic walkers report losing track of time and walking for much longer periods of time than they had planned. Since Nordic walking poles spread the effort of walking much more evenly throughout your body, you can walk for a long time before you feel it in your muscles. If you're planning to walk for an hour, prepare for a 75-minute workout!

The more you exercise outside, the higher your chances of acquiring an environmental injury. According to the Center for Disease Control in the U.S., little is known about the risk factors for many common recreational activities, including hiking, climbing, skiing, and riding vehicles like personal watercraft, snowmobiles, and all-terrain vehicles. Nordic walkers have the same risk factors as other outdoor athletes. You may sustain insect bites or accidental injuries, especially on varied terrain. Most outdoor-fitness injuries are due to exhaustion, overexertion, or climate-related illnesses.

Exercising in the Heat

Hot weather can compromise your performance. As your body's core temperature increases, your muscles may lose endurance. As you get used to the heat, you'll be able to train harder and tolerate hot weather better. Some experts say that it takes one to two weeks to acclimate to heat if you are not accustomed to it. Eventually, your body will adapt, with increased blood volume, more efficient sweating, lower core-body temperature, and lower heart-rate responses.

Hydration is key. In hot weather, your body dissipates its internal heat by sweating. Problems, such as heat cramps and heat exhaustion, arise when your body cannot release the internal heat or when the fluids lost through sweating are not replaced. You must hydrate your body to avoid heat stress and to improve the cellular functions that produce muscle contraction. Drink regularly, even if you don't feel thirsty. By the time you perceive your thirst, you may already be dehydrated. You should drink two cups (480 ml) of a

There are no limits to where you can Nordic walk, but remember to take safety precautions for different outdoor conditions.

beverage two hours before you exercise and 1 cup (240 ml) a few minutes before. Drink another 4 to 6 ounces (120-180 ml) every 15 minutes as you work out. If you are exercising in hot weather, choose water or sports drinks that help maintain performance with carbohydrate and electrolytes.

Nutrition is also important. Eating vegetables and fruits before exercising will help you maintain the trace minerals that are lost during sweating. The absence of these minerals causes heat cramps, or brief muscle contractions. If you sweat a lot or have problems with heat cramps, drink sport beverages containing sodium during and between bouts of exercise.

Here are some other guidelines for exercising in warmer weather:

- Wear lightweight, light-colored fabrics that wick away moisture. Nike Dri-Fit is a good choice. These fabrics promote ventilation and protect you from the sun's damaging rays.

- Wear sunscreen, a good pair of polarized sunglasses, and a hat to protect your face and eyes.

- Ease your body into the heat by decreasing the duration and intensity of your first few workouts.

- Avoid exercising during the warmest parts of the day. If you must go out in the middle of the day, choose a tree-lined path. Mornings and evenings are generally cooler.

- Hydrate! Drink a few ounces every 15 minutes.

- Pay attention to your heart rate. If your pulse is higher than it should be, taper back your walking intensity.

- Sleep loss, weight loss, and high humidity reduce your capacity for tolerating heat.

Exercising With Cold and Wind

Some Nordic walkers prefer cold weather because it's easier to regulate body temperatures. In fact, exercising in cold weather is healthy. Remember that the perception of cold is relative to your native climate. Someone who lives in southern climates might consider 50 degrees F (10 degrees C) to be cold, while another who works out in the mountains considers cold to be below freezing at 32 degrees F (0 degrees C). The distinction for safety is the difference between your body's internal temperature and the temperature outdoors.

Follow these tips to stay safe in cold weather:

- Dress in breathable layers, but do not overdress. Sweat combined with cold can lead to hypothermia, among other conditions. Wear synthetic fabrics next to your skin to wick moisture away from the body. Avoid cotton, which retains sweat like a sponge and sucks the heat out of your body. Wear a second layer of lightweight wool for warmth. The third layer of clothing should protect you from the wind.

- If the weather is below freezing temperatures, double your warm-up and cool-down times to protect your muscles and avoid chills due to excess perspiration after the workout.

- Hypothermia begins when the body's core temperature falls below 95 degrees F (35 degrees C). Symptoms include shivering and a rise in your blood pressure. If you stop shivering while outdoors, you must seek medical attention. This is a sign that your core temperature has dropped below 85 degrees F (30 degrees C). To avoid hypothermia, simply keep moving.

- Exercise-induced asthma, which results from dryness in the air, can occur in warm or cold weather at higher altitudes.

- When your internal temperature drops, your body attempts to regulate itself to preserve your organs. This can result in frostbite, a damaging lack of heat in distal areas like the nose, fingers, and toes.

- Even though you may not sweat in cold weather, your body still expels water through your nose and mouth (through breath or mucus), so remember to hydrate.

Exercising at High Altitude

Many athletes seek high-altitude training to improve the capacity of the blood to carry oxygen and to increase the presence of the chemical that makes oxygen available to the muscles. High altitude is also relative. For someone who lives at sea level, 3,000 feet (914 m) is very high, but someone who resides at 7,000 feet (2134 m) may consider 10,000 feet (3048 m) to be high. Your ability to work at altitude is based on your response to changes in pressure that limit your oxygen intake.

For endurance and high-intensity training, choose altitudes between 5,000 and 8,500 feet (1524-2591 m). In fact, living at that altitude is considered ideal. Compare your living environment with your fitness goals and your body's response to higher altitudes to find the best fit. If you want to compete at high altitudes, you should spend part of your time training there. If you live in a high-altitude area but want to increase your cardio capacity, spend time in both higher and lower altitudes.

Acclimatization can take four days to two weeks, depending on your fitness level and physiology. Symptoms of altitude sickness include loss of breath, dizziness, fatigue, nausea, headaches, and insomnia. Moving to higher altitudes reduces the body's capacity to deliver oxygen to the working muscles. Therefore, perform long, gradual warm-ups and cool-downs.

Safely Exercising Outdoors

- Wear the right gear.
- Follow general guidelines for working out safely: warm up, check your heart rate, cool down, and stretch.
- Enhance visual acuity. Instead of looking down at the ground, scan the area in front of you, looking all the way out to the horizon. This awareness helps you listen for traffic or other noises that indicate danger.
- Don't listen to loud music on busy paths and roads.
- Be familiar with your walking route.
- Bring a charged cell phone and wear a loud whistle. You may also want to learn some basic self-defense skills. You do have that carbide tip, after all!
- Tell someone where you're going and when you'll return. Better yet, take a friend along.
- Stay away from high-traffic walking areas!
- Hydrate.
- Wear a hat and sunscreen, regardless of the weather.
- Carry a small first-aid kit.

CHAPTER 7

Starting Up:
Identifying the
Workout for You

To identify effective workouts, this chapter discusses three categories of Nordic walkers: those working toward skill development, fitness proficiency, or competition. These three categories collectively represent a dynamic continuum (figure 7.1). Although you are stratified into a particular category when you first begin Nordic walking, you will likely progress from one category to the next as you continue training. Therefore, you should perform the assessments listed in this chapter every four to six weeks to determine if your category has changed. However, continuum changes are not necessary and should be made according to your goals. For example, if you enjoy fitness proficiency and feel motivated by the program, you may opt to remain there. On the other hand, if you seek a greater challenge and want a competitive edge, you are encouraged to progress to the competition category.

- *Skill development.* Use this training program if you are at a moderate level of fitness but need to focus on developing basic skills, including becoming comfortable with poles, walking with a natural gait, and using rhythmic movement of opposing arms and legs to enhance technique and efficiency. The workouts in chapters 8 and 9 are a great place to start.

- *Fitness proficiency.* Choose this training program if you are comfortable and have experience with Nordic walking poles. You should have the ability to instinctively move with relaxed precision and the technique to achieve a steady-state workout without contrived movement. The workouts in chapters 9 through12 provide appropriate challenges for this category. See also chapter 15 in part III, which focuses on total-body fitness.

• *Competition.* This training program advances beyond basic technique and efficiency of movement. You should be able to Nordic walk on multiple terrains using dynamic skills, such as lunging and bounding with poles. This level incorporates both steady-state and advanced anaerobic, interval-type training. Use this category if you want to train for endurance events such as half-marathons or marathons, or if you want to maintain a competitive edge for another sport. Chapters 10 through 13 provide a variety of suitable workouts for a comprehensive program, and chapters 16 and 17 provide cross-training workouts and guidelines for customized routines.

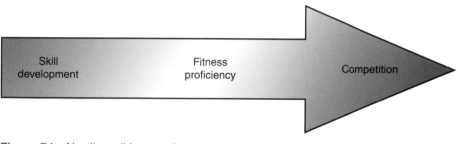

Figure 7.1   Nordic walking continuum.

Now that the categories have been outlined, consider how to determine the appropriate category for you.

Assessing Fitness Level

You should conduct several assessments to determine a good starting point before you Nordic walk into the sunset. These tools provide feedback about your current fitness level in terms of Nordic walking. One of the most motivating aspects of exercise is witnessing personal progress, so you should determine your starting point in order to measure your progress over time, gradually increase the level of difficulty, challenge and inspire yourself, and limit injury. Measure your fitness status every four to six weeks to determine if your body is ready for a new challenge.

The following questionnaire is a hybrid of health and fitness assessments, and can be conveniently self-administered (figure 7.2). It takes into account not only past and present Nordic walking levels, but also age, weight, illness, injuries, and even resting heart rate. This relatively comprehensive health and fitness questionnaire takes only a few minutes to complete and gives you an immediate rating of low, average, or high.

Nordic Walking Health/Fitness Assessment

Cardiovascular Health

Which of these statements best describes your cardiovascular condition? This is a critical safety check before you enter vigorous activity. Warning: If you have a cardiovascular disease history, start the walking programs in this book only after receiving clearance from your doctor, and then only with close supervision by a fitness instructor.

No history of heart or circulatory problems	_____ (3)
Past ailments treated successfully	_____ (2)
Such problems exist, but no treatment is required	_____ (1)
Under medical care for cardiovascular illness	_____ (0)

Injuries

Which of these statements best describes your current injuries? This is a test of your musculoskeletal readiness to start a walking program. Warning: If your injury is temporary, wait until it has healed before starting the program. If it is chronic, adjust the program to fit your limitations.

No current injury problems	_____ (3)
Some pain in activity, but not limited by it	_____ (2)
Level of activity limited by the injury	_____ (1)
Unable to do much strenuous training	_____ (0)

Illness

Which of these statements best describes your current illness? Certain temporary or chronic conditions will delay or disrupt your walking program.

No current illness problems	_____ (3)
Some problem in activity, but not limited by it	_____ (2)
Level of activity limited by the illness	_____ (1)
Unable to do much strenuous training	_____ (0)

Age

In which of these age groups do you fall? Generally, the younger you are, the less time you have spent slipping out of shape.

Age 20 or younger	_____ (3)
Age 21 to 29	_____ (2)
Age 30 to 39	_____ (1)
Age 40 and older	_____ (0)

Weight

Which of these ranges best describes how close you are to your own definition of ideal weight? Excess fat, which can be layered on thin people too, is a sign of unhealthy inactivity. Of course, being underweight isn't ideal either. Be honest.

Within 3 pounds of your own ideal weight	_____ (3)
Less than 10 pounds above or below your ideal weight	_____ (2)
11 to 19 pounds above or below your ideal weight	_____ (1)
20 or more pounds above or below your ideal weight	_____ (0)

Resting Pulse Rate

Which of these ranges describes your current resting pulse rate, your pulse upon waking in the morning before getting out of bed? The heart of a fit person normally beats more slowly and efficiently than an unfit heart.

Below 60 beats per minute	_____ (3)
61 to 69 beats per minute	_____ (2)
70 to 79 beats per minute	_____ (1)
80 or more beats per minute	_____ (0)

Smoking

Which of these statements describes your smoking history and current habits? Smoking is the major demon behind ill health that can be controlled.

Never a smoker	_____ (3)
Once a smoker, but quit	_____ (2)
An occasional, social smoker now	_____ (1)
A regular, heavy smoker now	_____ (0)

Most Recent Walk

Which of these statements best describes your walking within the last month? Your recent participation in a specific activity best predicts how you will do in the future.

Walked nonstop for more than 1 brisk mile	_____ (3)
Walked nonstop for 1/2 mile to 1 mile	_____ (2)
Walked less than 1/2 mile and took rests	_____ (1)
No recent walking of any distance	_____ (0)

Nordic Walking Background

Which of these statements best describes your Nordic walking history? Although fitness doesn't stick if you don't keep at it, if you once participated in an activity, you'll pick it up again more quickly.

Nordic walked regularly within the last year	_____ (3)
Nordic walked regularly one to two years ago	_____ (2)
Nordic walked regularly more than two years ago	_____ (1)
Never Nordic walked regularly	_____ (0)

(continued)

Nordic Walking Health/Fitness Assessment *(continued)*

Related Activities

Which of these statements best describes your participation in other aerobic activities? Continuous activities such as running, cross-country skiing, and bicycling help build a good foundation for other similar activities, such as Nordic walking. Nonaerobic activities, such as weightlifting and stop-and-go sports like tennis, don't contribute as much to the base conditioning needed.

Regularly practice continuous aerobic activity	_____ (3)
Sometimes practice continuous aerobic activity	_____ (2)
Practice nonaerobic or stop-and-go sports	_____ (1)
Not regularly active	_____ (0)
Total score	_____

Evaluate Your Score

≥20 points. You're high in overall health and fitness for a beginning Nordic walker. You could probably already handle 3- to 4-mile (4.8-6.4 km) walks at a steady clip, four or five days a week.

10-19 points. Your rating is average, which is a fine place to be. You could start by walking fewer days, perhaps no more than three a week, and could cover a maximum of 2 to 3 miles each time.

<10 points. Your score is low. You probably should start Nordic walking very short distances, for example, around the block a few times. Feel free to take plenty of breaks, building to 1 1/2 to 2 miles of easy Nordic walking that you can comfortably complete before you try a more challenging program.

Figure 7.2   Nordic Walking Health/Fitness Assessment.
Adapted, by permission, from T. Iknoian, 2005, *Fitness walking,* 2nd ed. (Champaign, IL: Human Kinetics), 10-12.

Now that the hand-to-paper exercise is finished, the walking assessment is next. Self-reported information based on memory, such as that used in the previous questionnaire, reflects only a piece of the puzzle. To determine a starting or progression point, you must also discover how your body responds to exercise in real time as this information is often times more valuable. You should trust your body's response, but you should also take into account the multiple variables that can influence heart rate and performance on any given day, such as fatigue, stress, dehydration, inadequate rest, and environmental influences. These microchanges determine which type of workout professional athletes or Olympians perform in daily training, and can certainly influence the outcome of competitions. Although the stakes may not be as high, recreational exercisers and athletes should also pay heed to any noticeable changes in their well-being and should respect their bodies accordingly. Observe the following considerations when performing the 1-mile walking test (figure 7.3).

Combine the results of the fitness assessment for walking health and the 1-mile walking test to determine which stage of training you are ready for (table 7.1).

If you score differently on each test and cannot reach a clear outcome, err on the conservative side and select the category with the lowest common denominator for your training. For example, if the fitness assessment for walking health places you into the low category, but the 1-mile walking test suggests you are average, you should still begin with the training program for skill development. Likewise, if your score is high on the fitness assessment but average on the walking test, begin training in the category of fitness proficiency.

1-Mile Walking Test

For safety, make sure someone is with you when you complete this evaluation.

1. For an exact distance, use a track or a measured and marked flat trail with a smooth surface. A standard track is 1/4 mile, so you will walk four laps in the inside lane for the 1-mile evaluation. Otherwise, use a measured path, a street you have measured with the odometer on your car, or a treadmill, all of which may be less accurate but close enough.

2. Warm up for several minutes with easy walking until your body feels warmer.

3. Get ready to start your mile walk. Tips: Try to walk a pace that's steady but feels as if you're pushing hard. Remember, you'll probably walk at least 11 to 14 minutes, so don't start too fast. Pick up the pace in the last couple of minutes or last lap if you feel strong, which you should if you don't start too fast.

4. Your goal is to feel tired but not exhausted. You should feel slightly winded, but you should not gasp and pant (RPE 7-8, see page 122).

5. Cool down by continuing to walk slowly for a few minutes after you are done, then stretch.

6. Compare your time to the chart to assess your classification.

Minutes Walking		
Men	Women	Fitness Classification
>16:00	>17:00	Beginner
13:00-16:00	14:00-17:00	Average
<13:00	<14:00	Advanced

Figure 7.3 1-Mile Walking Test.
Adapted, by permission, from T. Iknoian, 2005, *Fitness walking,* 2nd ed. (Champaign, IL: Human Kinetics), 13.

Table 7.1   Training Breakdown for Nordic Walking

Fitness assessment	1-mile walking test	Training program for Nordic walking
Low	Beginner	Skill development
Average	Average	Fitness proficiency
High	Advanced	Competition

Choosing the Right Workout

Once you have identified a training program, use the following guidelines from the FITT (frequency, intensity, time, and type) principle as a general guide, referencing specific training workouts from part II. If your long-term goals are already clear, consult part III for routines that are geared for specific outcomes.

Generally speaking, if you are looking for an outline of structured workouts for skill development, begin with the short and easy workouts in chapter 8. If your fitness level is higher than your skill level for Nordic walking, choose the medium and steady workouts from chapter 9, which provide a good balance of technique refinement and cardiorespiratory challenge. If you are forming long-term training goals, see chapter 14 for additional routines for cardiorespiratory health and fitness. As in any new activity, be patient; don't progress to the next level until you have developed a base of solid technique in your current practice.

If your scores indicate that you have a good balance of technique and fitness, begin with the medium and steady workouts from chapter 9, but consider incorporating workouts from chapters 10 through 12 to keep your program diverse. You should change the intensity of your program from day to day to allow for proper recovery. Keep your program fresh while following the FITT principle by picking workouts from each category.

If you fall into the category for competitive training, prepare for a dynamic routine that pushes the limits of Nordic walking. As with any challenging exercise program, you must take care not to overtrain when setting aggressive personal goals. All of the workouts in part II are fair game, but be sure that you don't focus solely on high-intensity workouts. Look at chapter 13, which outlines exciting outdoor workouts. If you're Nordic walking in conjunction with another sport, see chapter 16 for great nuggets of information that will keep any workout lively. The FITT principle provides good basic guidelines, but if you want a creative and customized workout, chapter 17 provides great recommendations based on periodization training.

Guidelines for Optimal Cardiovascular Endurance Progression: The FITT Principle

You must choose an appropriate rate of exercise progression to ensure that desired improvements are achieved and that health issues and injuries do not arise. Unfortunately, many people believe that cardiorespiratory routines can be started and stopped abruptly, and that workouts that are longer and more frequent must be better. Would you consider doing squats with a straight bar loaded with 200 pounds (91 kg) of free weights without first warming up? Do you think it is healthy to perform six sets of 15 repetitions the first time you attempt an exercise? Hopefully, your answer is no. You should apply the same principle to Nordic walking. If given the opportunity, your body can adapt to accomplish amazing feats, but you must exercise patience, discipline, and intelligence when planning your program.

In the field of exercise physiology, the FITT principle is one of the guiding ideas for proper exercise progression. It outlines the quantifiable components of an exercise routine: frequency, intensity, time, and type of exercise. You can use this principle as an umbrella for all types of programming. Part II details specific workouts that can be used as part of your overall plan.

Nordic walking is a great way to improve fitness, but make your improvements gradually to be safe.

- *Frequency.* Healthy adults should exercise three to five days per week to improve and maintain cardiorespiratory fitness. Beginning Nordic walkers who are working on skill development should aim for at least three days per week, but those who are working on fitness proficiency and competition should exercise three to five days each week. There is typically no improvement with exercise frequencies greater than fives days a week, and it may even increase injury risk. However, if there is a variety of cross-training activites performed in which different muscle groups are used then it may be recommended.

- *Intensity.* To improve cardiorespiratory fitness in healthy adults, the recommended intensity is between 57 and 94 percent of maximum heart rate (see HRmax on page 121). Nordic walkers who are working on skill development should aim for moderate intensities of 57 to 84 percent of HRmax, and those in the other two categories should aim for a HRmax that is a combination of moderate intensity with vigorous intensity (between 80 and 94 percent).

- *Time.* To improve cardiorespiratory fitness in healthy adults, the duration of exercise should be at least 20 to 90 minutes. Beginning Nordic walkers should exercise for at least 30 minutes at a moderate intensity working towards 150 minutes per week. Those in the more advanced categories should aim to work out for at least 20 minutes at vigorous intensity, to 90 minutes and above at moderate intensity for a total between 200-300 minutes per week.

- *Type.* Exercises that are continuous and dynamic, and that stimulate large muscle groups are required to improve cardiorespiratory fitness. Nordic walking is a perfect example, as are cycling, swimming, running, in-line skating and cross-country skiing. Beginners who are working on skill development should Nordic walk three days each week, and those in the other two categories may want to cross-train with another cardiorespiratory exercise one to two days per week.

Guidelines for Warming Up and Cooling Down

As in any athletic endeavor, you must warm up prior to exercising to prepare your body for the upcoming challenge. A gradual warm-up does precisely what the word suggests; it increases the temperature of deep muscles and the body's core. The rise in temperature also stimulates heart rate, respiration, viscosity of joint fluids, and perspiration, which translates into greater readiness to perform. In addition, a proper warm-up reduces the potential for muscle stiffness and soreness after the routine is over. You can accomplish all of this by merely performing at least 5 to 10 minutes of cardiovascular and muscular endurance activity-specific movement as outlined in the following section.

Often overlooked but equally important, a cool-down period tells the body that the work is over and helps it recover. A gradual cool-down moves blood through the muscles and back to the working heart. Keeping the oxygen-rich blood moving minimizes soreness and stiffness, particularly after an intense workout. To facilitate the cool-down process, lower the intensity of the activity while stretching as described in the next section.

Warm-Ups

Since warm-ups consist of low-intensity activity, continuous movement, and limited range of motion, they don't require sets. Table 7.2 lists specific exercises to use. This time is not intended to be difficult.

A general warm-up for Nordic walking can simply consist of walking slowly with poles for five minutes. More intense and longer workouts require a longer warm-up. Finish the warm-up with dynamic activity-specific movements, such as leg swings and partner choo-choo train in chapter 5 (pages 84 and 77 respectively). These movements should take you through a fluid full range of motion. Take time to work up to the speed and rhythm that your Nordic walking pace requires. Typically, the more rigorous your workout is, the more time you should spend doing both general and activity-specific movements to simulate the intensity and prepare your muscles and joints for what is to come.

Limbering, which takes only a few minutes, is the process of loosening up your muscles. To perform shoulder rolls, stand upright, holding the poles in front of you and parallel to the ground. Roll your shoulders backward and forward 10 times. Next, do 10 chest stretches. Hold the individual poles vertically in front of your body. Keep your elbows soft, your arms outstretched,

Table 7.2   Warm-Up Exercises

Exercise	Time	Repetitions
Flex and extend ankles		10 per side
Single-side balance	20-60 sec per side	
Leverage lower leg		10 per side
Squats		10
Standing leg lifts		10 per side
Multidirectional arm raises		10

Directions for these exercises are presented in chapters 4 and 5.

and your hands level with your shoulders. Bring your arms together in front to open your back, and then reverse the movement, leading with slightly bent elbows, to open your chest. Finally, do 10 standing torso twists. Place the poles on top of your shoulders and rest your hands on either end. Assume a stance a bit wider than your hips, soften your knees, and slowly rotate your torso to the right and left. Do not complete a full range of motion. Move through half of your range during warm-ups.

Dynamic stretching, also considered unassisted movement since it does not require a partner, has been shown to have some benefits when performed as part of the warm-up period. The term typically refers to a bouncing move that creates a stretch, but dynamic stretches actively move the joints in a way that is specific to Nordic walking. For example, to enhance torso flexibility, hold poles at a horizontal position that is shoulder's width apart while rotating the trunk. Dynamic stretches can be done prior to exercise since they simulate the motion of the planned activity. Perform these movements in a controlled manner without ballistic movement. You can also use these stretches after the activity as long as you use slower movements to signal your body that it is time to cool down.

As with other elements of fitness, there are specific guidelines for stretching to maximize the benefits. Stretching programs can benefit from the FITT principle as well: Frequency, Intensity, Time and Type. Stretching should be performed at a frequency of least 2 to 3 days a week, but ideally 5 to 7 days a week. Intensity is an important marker for stretching. A stretch should be held only until muscles feel tight rather than to a point of pain. In terms of time, stretches should be held for 15 to 60 seconds. Each stretch should be repeated at least 3 times per muscle group, with a rest period of 20 to 30 seconds in between. Preferably after activity or appropriate warm-up period, the recommended types of stretching that should be done are in the form of static, dynamic, or PNF (proprioceptive neuromuscular fascilitation), which are described in more detail below.

Contrary to popular belief, stationary (static) stretching and warming up are not one and the same. In the traditional sense, stationary stretching does not necessarily prepare the muscles and joints for dynamic movement. In fact, some research in the last decade suggests that static stretching before activity may compromise performance, weaken the muscles, and reduce their ability to produce force. This pertains to resistance training and endurance exercise, particularly if you're doing a high-intensity routine that includes bounding or intervals. In this case stationary stretching is best done after the session.

There is no conclusive evidence that stretching before activity improves performance or prevents injury. However, it is not certain that stretching prior to exercise is detrimental for those pursuing general fitness or when used for activities that require greater flexibility. In this case, although it is appropriate for some to stretch after the warm-up, for the purpose of continuity of the information in this book, we recommend stretching after the cool-down.

As explained above, the following stationary stretches are examples that are optional, and encouraged during the cool-down period. These active and unassisted stretches involve slow, controlled movements that create mild muscle tension. Stretch until you have a feeling of slight discomfort and hold the position for 15 to 60 seconds. Some research shows that holding the stretch longer increases your flexibility over time.

Cool-Downs

Cool-down periods help the body transition both physiologically and psychologically from the stress of exercise to a state of rest. Gradually decreasing the intensity to a mild level for approximately five minutes circulates a large volume of blood from the working muscles back to the heart. Allowing the heart rate and blood pressure to decrease slowly also helps the muscles eliminate waste products. Some people routinely end a workout session by jumping into the shower or into a car, but this practice can be dangerous. Blood can pool in the legs instead of circulating back to the heart, leading to dizziness or even fainting. A cool-down period can also help you get back into a relaxed psychological mind-set.

As previously mentioned, current research indicates that stretching is most effective for enhancing flexibility and recovery when done as part of the cool-down period. Flexibility is helpful for athletes who want to experience general ease of joint movement, and a full range of motion during exercise. Stretching can improve flexibility by as much as 20 percent over a period of several weeks. However, flexibility can also decrease within three to four weeks if not maintained.

In addition to the stationary and dynamic stretches previously mentioned, PNF (proprioceptive neuromuscular facilitation) has been found to be equally effective for increasing flexibility when the muscles are warm. PNF stretching is a method that was originally developed as part of a neuromuscular rehabilitation program to relax muscles. It is considered passive or assisted, requiring a partner or a tool such as a towel or piece of tubing. Therefore, is not always the most practical way to end an exercise session. Research has not yet determined whether PNF is superior to stationary stretching, so the choice is up to you. The following section outlines a variety of PNF styles.

Figure 7.4   Hold-relax stretching technique.

There are three types of PNF stretches: hold-relax, contract-relax, and hold-relax with agonist contraction. Figure 7.4*a-b* shows the first hold-relax technique for the hamstring (back of the thigh), which begins with a passive prestretch that is held for 10 seconds. As your partner applies mild force, hold your leg in an isometric contraction (don't allow the joints to move) for approximately six seconds. Relax, and then perform another passive stretch with a partner for 10 to 30 seconds. You should feel yourself settling much deeper into the stretch.

The contract-relax technique (figure 7.5) for the hamstring (back of the thigh) also begins with a passive stretch for 10 seconds. However, this time you should apply force using the muscle on the back of your thigh as your partner moves your joint through the range of motion during your concentric muscle contraction lasting six seconds. As in the first technique, the final passive stretch should be performed for 10 to 30 seconds without resistance. You should be able to feel an improvement.

The final technique, hold-relax with agonist contraction, appears to be the most effective (figure 7.6). Also for the hamstring (back of the thigh), the first

Figure 7.5   Contract-relax stretching technique.

Figure 7.6   Hold-relax with agonist contraction stretching technique.

two steps are the same as in the hold-relax technique. However, in the third phase you should contract the muscle opposite (agonist) to the one that your partner is stretching for you for 10 to 30 seconds. For example, in this stretch you should contract your hip and thigh in the opposite direction your partner is moving your leg. This practice adds force, resulting in a greater overall stretch. Although these methods require a partner and more time, many athletes consider them the most effective way to enhance flexibility.

Assessing Pace and Intensity

Certain factors can vary to fit the needs of the exercise being performed. The variable components of Nordic walking are pace and intensity. Many competitive athletes enjoy taking measurements during workouts to obtain immediate feedback and work toward future goals. The following information provides resources for getting immediate and long-term feedback.

Pace

Pace can either refer to the length of your step or the speed at which you step. This book refers to pace as the rate at which you Nordic walk. You can measure your pace by wearing a GPS unit on your wrist that instantly calculates your speed (usually in miles per hour). Use table 7.3 to determine your steps per minute and minutes per mile (or km). However, most individuals use other methods.

For the most basic method, you must have knowledge of two out of three categories: distance, time, and speed. The easiest method is to measure the distance of your route, and then divide the number by the number of minutes it took you to complete it. Finally, multiply the sum by 60 to find your speed in miles per hour (miles ÷ time in minutes × 60 = mph). Use table 7.3 to determine your steps per minute and minutes per mile.

Table 7.3   Estimating Your Pace With Steps per Minute

Steps/min	Miles/hour	Min/mile
60-80	2-2.4	25-30
85-95	2.5-2.9	21-24
100-115	3-3.3	18-20
120-125	3.4-3.6	16-17
130-135	3.8-4	15-16
140-145	4.3-4.6	13-14
150-155	4.6-4.8	12-13
160-165	5-5.2	11-12
170+	>5.5	<11

Adapted, by permission, from T. Iknoian, 2005, *Fitness walking,* 2nd ed. (Champaign, IL: Human Kinetics), 43.

If you do not know your distance, identify your steps per minute and consult table 7.3. Most people do not have the patience or drive to count steps for a minute, so the easiest method is to use either a pedometer or an accelerometer. See chapter 2 for more information on both tools.

Intensity

Although this book names intensity in terms of maximum heart rate (HRmax), multiple methods for measuring the intensity of exercise exist. The following section describes the most commonly used methods.

Maximum Heart Rate

One of the simplest ways of determining intensity is to calculate a range based on a percentage of your maximum heart rate. Most commercial cardiorespiratory machines use the classic method to estimate your target heart rate based on your age. This classic method simply subtracts age from 220 beats per minute to estimate maximal heart rate. However, this underestimates maximal heart rate in those younger than the age of 40, and overestimates it in those older than 40. A more accurate method of predicting maximal heart rate requires an extra calculation, but is more appropriate for all ages. To calculate an estimate of your HRmax, begin by multiplying 0.67 by your age. Next, subtract the result from 206.9.

$$HRmax = 206.9 - (0.67 \times age)$$

Next, to calculate target heart rate multiply the intensity (number in terms of percentage) you desire by your HRmax. For example, if your calculated HRmax is 180 bpm and you want to exercise at 70 percent of your HRmax, then multiply .70 by 180 to get 126 bpm.

$$THR = Desired \% \times HRmax$$

If you would like a more accurate estimate that takes into account your current fitness level, use the heart-rate reserve method below.

Heart-Rate Reserve (HRR)

The method for heart-rate reserve (HRR), also known as Karvonen's method, involves a few more calculations. It is often considered more accurate than other methods. To perform this calculation, obtain an accurate resting heart rate (HRrest). The best time to measure your resting heart rate is in the morning before you get out of bed. This practice ensures that your heart rate doesn't suddenly increase. Locate your pulse under your wrist on the thumb side, hold your first two fingers to the spot, and then count for 60 seconds.

$$HRR = HRmax - HRrest \times \% HRmax + HRrest$$

Step 1: Measure resting heart rate (HRrest)

Step 2: 206.9 − (0.67 × age) = maximum heart rate (HRmax)

Step 3: HRmax − HRrest × percent of desired intensity (% HRmax)
+ HRrest = HRR

Example: 45-year-old male in the fitness proficiency category who desires 75 to 90 percent HRmax

Step 1: HRrest = 65

Step 2: 206.9 − (0.67 × 45) = 176.8 HRmax

Step 3: (176.8 − 65) × .75 (75%) + 65 = 148.9; (176.8 − 65) × .9 (90%) + 65 = 165.6

Result: The exerciser's heart rate should remain between 149 and 166 beats per minute (bpm), which represents 75 to 90 percent of HRmax.

Note: This method more accurately estimates exercise intensity because it factors in resting heart rate, an indication of current fitness level.

Assessing Intensity

Once you have calculated the range for your target heart rate, measure your intensity while exercising to ensure a safe and effective workout. You can accomplish this by measuring your heart rate or by calculating your rating of perceived exertion (RPE).

Monitoring Heart Rate   You can easily measure your heart rate by wearing a heart rate monitor. These devices, which generally range in price from $40 to $300, are worn around the chest or wrist to capture a pulse. Both versions are fun and easy to use. The most basic models measure heart rate alone, while the GPS model can measure calories burned, speed, distance, temperature, and even altitude. Most models have an alarm that sounds to keep you within the zone of your target heart rate.

The alternative is to measure your pulse manually. Although this method is free, it is often less convenient. Measuring a pulse while exercising can be difficult because movement from activity is sometimes confused with the pulse. The best way to successfully detect your heart beat is to stop your activity completely. However, heart rate slows with every few seconds of inactivity, which lessens the accuracy of the reading. Therefore for a quick reading, simply place your index and forefinger under your wrist on the thumb side, count the number of beats in 6 seconds, and then multiply that number by ten to determine your heart rate per minute.

Rating of Perceived Exertion (RPE)   Another method for determining your exercise intensity is with a subjective tool called the rating of perceived exertion (RPE). As the name suggests, you assign a number to describe how hard you feel you are working which correlates well with exercise heart rate. One common rating scale, called Borg's Category-Ratio Scale, asks you to identify a number between 0 and 10. Specifically, assign a rating of 0 for what you may experience if you were sitting in a chair, 2 for light activity, 5 for heavy activity, and 10 for maximal intensity. Take note that your rating can be influenced by mood, environmental conditions, and the type of exercise. In the absence of an objective heart rate monitor, this tool is invaluable, particularly if you know your body well. You can use it in conjunction with a heart rate monitor. However, it is important to pay attention to what your body is saying, sometimes even in spite of your heart rate.

For example, if your goal for the day is to exercise in a heart-rate zone between 80 and 90 percent but you feel extremely fatigued, you should modify the workout accordingly and take a lower-intensity recovery day. RPE is also a great tool for people taking cholesterol medication that suppresses heart-rate response, which renders the method for heart-rate training inaccurate. In this case, use RPE as the primary guide for intensity. Table 7.4 shows the correlation between RPE and heart rate. Additionally, different intensity levels correspond to specific workouts from part II. This table does not list speed or terrain, since the workouts are detailed by type in part II.

Table 7.4　Intensity Levels for Walking Workouts

Workout type (see part II)	RPE	% HRmax
Short and easy	1-5	55-75
Medium and steady	3-7	60-80
Medium and quick	4-8	65-85
Short and fast	5-8	75-89
Long and steady	5-8	75-89
Freestyle and boot-camp circuit training	4-9	65-94

Components of Exercise Progression

In addition to the general guidelines listed previously, consider the following guidelines for progressing your exercise routine over time. These considerations are based on current fitness level, age, activity preferences, goals, injury status, and tolerance to training. You should progress gradually, particularly if you are new to Nordic walking.

- *Initiation stage (4 to 6 weeks).* This stage is important if you already have a moderate level of fitness yet are new to Nordic walking, highlighting lower-intensity workouts of shorter duration to minimize soreness. To progress, a good rule of thumb is to increase your exercise session duration by 5 to 10 minutes every one to two weeks. Remember to warm up and cool down appropriately.

- *Improvement (next 4 to 8 months).* This stage incorporates the principle of progressive overload, in which improvements in cardiorespiratory fitness require incremental challenges. These challenges can be defined by increases in frequency, intensity, and duration of exercise. To accomplish this, the total volume of training (frequency $\times$ intensity $\times$ duration) should not increase more than 10 percent each week. You should gradually build your intensity up to 60 to 90 percent HRmax. Increasing both intensity and duration within an exercise session is not ideal. You must pay attention to signals from your body that may indicate overtraining, such as chronic soreness, fatigue, disinterest in exercise, irritability, or elevated resting heart rate. If you develop these symptoms, decrease the volume of your workouts and take more recovery days. Revisit the fitness assessments from this chapter to measure improvements in fitness and skill development.

• *Maintenance (longer than 6 months).* Once you have reached the fitness level you desire, focus on maintaining your progress without backsliding. See chapter 16 for information on cross-training, which keeps your routine fresh and your motivation high. Your body will also be pleased, since cross-training prevents overuse of particular muscles and joints. This is also a good time to reevaluate your need for gear or equipment. If you want more diversity in your workout or would like to set longer-term goals, consider the periodization principles discussed in chapter 17.

PART II

Nordic Walking Workouts

CHAPTER 8

Short and Easy

Several years ago, it was thought that you could not benefit from workouts shorter than an hour. We now know this is not the case. The guidelines of the ACSM indicate that shorter workouts, with consistent frequency and duration, can develop cardiorespiratory endurance, strength, and flexibility. Of course, the more time you dedicate to fitness practices, the healthier you become.

These short and easy workouts provide options for when time and good intentions slip by. They are also ideal for easing back into fitness. In order to achieve fitness with Nordic walking, you must safely increase your intensity when training and learning skills. The potential for injury increases when you use equipment with inefficient technique. If you have never Nordic walked before, take a lesson from a qualified instructor. Consider it a warm-up for your nervous system that will help your body adapt to using new equipment.

These workouts give beginners who are moderately fit enough time to become proficient at skills before the pace and intensity increase. These workouts are simple enough for beginners and can serve as great warm-ups or recovery-day workouts for athletes doing heavier training.

The objective of this chapter is to help you ease into walking with intensity, improve your skills at a comfortable pace, and find a comfortable stride length. You can injure yourself by trying to use longer strides too fast and too soon. Chapter 3 outlines skill progressions in more detail, but here is a quick reminder of how to achieve a proper and efficient stride:

1. Get into a rhythm of moving your arms and legs in opposition.
2. Extend your arms in front to lengthen your legs.
3. By default, the extension of your limbs creates a longer stride.

Workouts last 20 to 60 minutes, not including warm-up and cool-down times. These first eight workouts are based on time. Since stride length varies from one walker to another, don't measure your distance until you have established a base level of proficiency, which takes time and practice. Choose paved or dirt surfaces to help you ease into fitness with Nordic walking. You should achieve an RPE of 1 to 5 and a maximum heart rate of 55 to 75 percent.

We do not want you to rush to learn these skills. Going slowly at the beginning will help you speed up in the long run. By performing the skills sequentially and individually, you will become more efficient.

All workouts in this chapter begin with five to eight minutes of warm-ups that include a combination of balance exercises, limbering movements, and leisurely Nordic walking. Since most of these workouts are lower in intensity, you should cool down with five to eight minutes of slow walking and stretching (see chapter 7).

The warm-up helps you tune into the natural mechanisms that prime your muscles for effort and your body enters the fast lane of learning and efficiency.

The warm-up consists of two basic parts:

1. *Easy walking.* Take a few minutes to walk at a very comfortable pace and ease into the Nordic workout.
2. *Limbering.* Loosening up the limbs by bending and flexing, which enables free and easy movement.

These timed workouts allow you to focus on two primary elements of development: technique (proficiency of movement) and endurance. Subsequent chapters present distance workouts. Workouts in part II vary in time and distance, but each one presents an objective and provides tips to help you reach it. See chapter 3 for specific details about Nordic walking skills. All the workouts in this book are presented in a progressive and logical order that will help you transform from a weekend walker into a marathon charger!

Terrain in these workouts consists of paved and dirt roads that are mostly flat, but some have gradual inclines. Explore your potential by practicing with both tips on varied surfaces. Exercising in dirt can be a wholesome, rich experience that primes the nervous system for new learning. Walking on natural surfaces forces your feet and ankles to make subtle changes to maintain balance.

Although they are simple, the workouts in this chapter take you from beginner to skilled walker in eight weeks. They will challenge you to learn to use the poles not for stability, but to move forward smoothly and quickly. By the end of this chapter, even if your skills are not yet perfect, you will feel comfortable using the poles for the process of Nordic walking.

However, if you are pregnant or injured, you may need the poles more for stability than forward propulsion. In these cases, you may not be able to use the tips to push you forward from behind. Rather, you may need to walk with the tips in front for the duration of your pregnancy or recovery. In particular, workout 1 is recommended for those rehabilitating from injury.

Preview: Short and Easy Workouts

Workout	Walking time (min)	Terrain	Pace	Intensity (% HRmax / RPE)
1	20	Flat/paved	Easy	55-60 / 1-2
2	30	Flat/paved	Easy	55-60 / 2
3	25	Flat/paved	Easy/moderate	55-65 / 2-3
4	35	Flat/dirt	Easy/moderate	55-65 / 2-3
5	30	Flat/paved/ gradual incline	Easy/moderate	55-70 / 3
6	40	Flat/paved/ gradual incline	Easy/moderate	55-70 / 3-4
7	60	Flat/dirt	Moderate	65-75 / 4-5
8	50	Flat/paved	Moderate	60-75 / 3-5

Workout 1

Objective: Whether you are an injured athlete patiently doing everything right in the recovery process or someone who hasn't exercised as often as you should, your task in this workout is the same: just go! Don't make pace the priority. Instead, concentrate on how it feels to step methodically from one foot to the other. Every step gets you closer to your goal.

Time	20 minutes
Terrain	Flat, paved surface
Pace	Easy
Intensity	55 to 60 percent HRmax
RPE	1 to 2

Skill Focus: Walk and Swing harnesses the most fundamental element of Nordic walking: the opposing swing of arms and legs. Use this focus to establish a new sense of your body's rhythmic nature!

Comments: Move at a casual pace that gives you time to properly practice your skills. If you feel like taking a break, slow down, but keep walking. After a few minutes, resume your previous pace. You should never feel uncomfortable.

Workout 2

Objective: This workout is a little longer than the last one, but the intensity is the same. Use the time to your benefit. This low-stress workout is a good option for pregnant women who are in the habit of working out. Continue to practice walking and swinging, adding postural awareness to your technique. See chapter 3 for more details.

Time	30 minutes
Terrain	Flat, paved surface
Pace	Easy
Intensity	55 to 60 percent HRmax
RPE	2

Skill Focus: Instructors frequently reference the skill set highlighted in Walk and Swing because this seemingly mechanical automation of movements is essential for establishing a natural walking rhythm. You must master these basic skills before progressing to the next step. Your patience will pay off!

Comments: It is not appropriate for pregnant women to assume an athletic, wide stride because pregnancy changes the texture and elasticity of the body's connective tissues.

Workout 3

Objective: As you feel comfortable, increase your level of exertion to assume a moderate pace. This process should happen naturally when you are ready to move with more efficiency.

Time	25 minutes
Terrain	Flat, paved surface
Pace	Easy to moderate
Intensity	55 to 65 percent HRmax
RPE	2 to 3

Skill Focus: From this point forward, start your workout with Walk and Swing to establish a rhythm. Next, use Long Arms to improve your technique and stride. Focus on the forward swing of your arms to develop a longer lever that originates from the shoulders.

Comments: Be aware of the length of your arms as you stride. Ask a friend to watch from the side and to evaluate whether you are walking with arm levers that are short and bent or long and outstretched.

Workout 4

Objective: Congratulations on venturing out on dirt roads for the first time! Concentrate on the tips and handles of the poles as you encounter small rocks and uneven surfaces that may challenge your balance.

Time	35 minutes
Terrain	Flat, dirt surface
Pace	Easy to moderate
Intensity	55 to 65 percent HRmax
RPE	2 to 3

Skill Focus: Remove the rubber tips of the poles to reveal the sturdy carbide point beneath. Anchor the rubber tip between the balls of your feet, angle the pole slightly to the right to avoid hitting yourself in the chin, and then pull the pole upward. The rubber tip should remain on the ground between your feet.

Comments: You may find the carbide tips easier to use because they feel lighter. Additionally, you never need to worry about which way your tips are pointing. The cupping technique helps you develop your grip strength as your stride progresses.

Workout 5

Objective: Walk confidently up your first hill. Use the poles for support on the incline. Also, work on your cadence and stride length.

Time	30 minutes
Terrain	Flat, paved surface with gradual incline
Pace	Easy to moderate
Intensity	55 to 70 percent HRmax
RPE	3

Skill Focus: Your objective is to move your arms and legs with the same cadence and timing. Focus on stride development as you swing your legs forward from the hips. A longer stride is better because it offsets the tendency to lead with the head and shoulders, which can strain the lower back.

Comments: Walk for 10 minutes on a flat surface and then find a very gradual incline. Keep your chin level with the angle of the walking surface to protect your lower back as you move uphill. Concentrate on moving with long arms and legs, extending the length of your swing by 1 inch (2.5 cm). Your left arm and your right leg should simultaneously swing forward at the same speed.

Workout 6

Objective: This workout, which jazzes things up and loosens you up, focuses on spine rotation, arm extension, and tip contact.

Time	40 minutes
Terrain	Flat, paved surface with gradual incline
Pace	Easy to moderate
Intensity	55 to 70 percent HRmax
RPE	3 to 4

Skill Focus: When a tip meets the walking surface, it acts like a momentary anchor for your arm and the corresponding side of your upper torso, rotating your shoulder backward as you move. As you move your opposite hand and shoulder forward, your spine rotates.

Comments: You can also rotate your spine by exaggerating the placement of your feet. As you walk, practice crossing one foot in front of the other as if you were trying out for the TV show, *America's Next Top Model.* This drill immediately complements the movements of your upper body to create counterrotation. Find your stride as you approach the hill, then maintain the same pace and level of rotation as you climb up. Take longer strides for greater intensity.

Workout 7

Objective: This workout, which is the longest in this chapter, enhances your endurance and aerobic capacity. Increase intensity by using the tip as a resistance tool to help you move faster and lengthen your stride.

Time	60 minutes
Terrain	Flat, dirt surface
Pace	Moderate
Intensity	65 to 75 percent HRmax
RPE	4 to 5

Skill Focus: Focus on engaging the tip, which combines all the skills you have learned so far and takes cupping to a new level. When you feel the pole make contact with the ground, cup the handles and press through the tips, which must be placed to the sides or behind the body.

Comments: Be wary of rushing to master this skill and forcing your body to speed up before it is ready. After all, you must practice Nordic walking for eight weeks before you feel proficient. Take the last week to work on this skill.

Workout 8

Objective: This simple and classic workout is the backbone of Nordic walking fitness. Focus on putting all the skills you have learned to use and walking steadily!

Time	50 minutes
Terrain	Flat, paved surface
Pace	Moderate
Intensity	60 to 75 percent HRmax
RPE	3 to 5

Skill Focus: No additional skills are required for this workout. If anything, don't think, just walk.

Comments: The steady walking patterns of the previous workouts have enhanced your level of aerobic fitness. The RPE is a little higher, so strive for endurance!

CHAPTER 9

Medium and Steady

When you make Nordic walking a staple of your fitness training, all of its benefits become more apparent, especially its cardiorespiratory nature. The addictive quality of endorphins that are produced by performing repetitive, rhythmic movements over distance and time also stands out. Use this chapter if you have mastered the skills put forth in chapter 8.

The experience of Nordic walking is often compared to the classic runner's high, or the physical euphoria that takes place only when the joints have sustained activity over a period of time. More joint activity means more muscle involvement. The combination of skill-minded practice and longer workouts allows your muscles to learn more efficiently. The meditative state induced by endorphins will help you walk longer and build endurance, the prerequisite for success as your training goals become more intense.

This chapter outlines steady-state workouts that are heavenly for the fitness-minded walker, with options for simply walking or improving skills on varied terrain. Medium and steady workouts will help you enhance cardio fitness, continue developing technique, and focus purely on walking. You cannot practice enough if you want to walk or run into your golden years.

The following eight workouts are similar to those presented in chapter 8, but are longer and progressively more intense. Medium and steady workouts are ideal if you can devote 50 to 75 minutes to working out in an RPE range of 3 to 7. You will love these workouts if you wish to lose weight, since the higher RPE will kickstart your metabolism and burn greater amounts of fat.

Your maximum heart rate should range from 60 to 80 percent. As in chapter 8, you should choose flat paved or dirt paths that keep training simple.

Assuming that you have practiced enough to become proficient, you should start to take distance seriously. You can measure the distance of your route by driving it in your car and watching the odometer or by walking with a high-tech pedometer. Next, use a couple of these workouts to measure your distance against your time. In other words, identify a distance you think you can finish in a certain time, say 50 minutes. Walk for 50 minutes to see if you accomplish your target distance. If not, pay attention to how far you can comfortably walk in 50 minutes. These workouts aim to enhance cardiorespiratory fitness and to gradually increase RPE and working heart rate so you can work on training goals that are more intense in the future.

Preview: Medium and Steady Workouts

Workout	Walking time (min)	Terrain	Pace	Intensity (% HRmax / RPE)
1	50	Flat/paved	Moderate	60-70 / 3-4
2	50	Flat/dirt	Moderate	60-75 / 3-5
3	60	Flat/paved	Moderate	65-75 / 4-5
4	60	Flat/dirt/moderate incline	Moderate	65-75 / 4-5
5	60	Flat/paved	Moderate	70-77 / 5-6
6	75	Flat/dirt	Moderate	70-75 / 5
7	75	Paved/rolling hills	Moderate	65-77 / 4-6
8	60	Flat/dirt	Moderate/fast	70-80 / 5-7

Workout 1

Objective: Often, the rhythmic groove of a cardio workout temporarily distracts from any physical pain or discomfort you may be experiencing. Use the steady pace of this workout to simply pay attention to the sensations of your body.

Time	50 minutes
Terrain	Flat, paved surface
Pace	Moderate
Intensity	60 to 70 percent HRmax
RPE	3 to 4

Fitness Focus: As you walk, assess your body's movement from the feet up. Do you feel any physical discomfort or pain as you move? To improve your technique, concentrate more on your joints than on your muscles. Are you moving with symmetry? Your goal in this drill is to become more aware of your body for greater efficiency of movement.

Comments: With a length of 50 minutes, this workout is ideal for lunch time. The mellow and constant intensity provides steady and continuous aerobic conditioning and helps you clear your mind. The moderate pace gives you the opportunity to polish your skills.

Workout 2

Objective: Go outdoors and find somewhere new! You may discover an unexplored dirt road that is closer to home.

Time	50 minutes
Terrain	Flat, dirt surface
Pace	Moderate
Intensity	60 to 75 percent HRmax
RPE	3 to 5

Fitness Focus: Appreciating nature is as good for your head as it is for your body. As you continue working on your skills, pay attention to any sounds that are not man-made.

Comments: If you live in the U.S., contact the local Bureau of Land Management, Forest Service, or Department of Agriculture for a free map of accessible dirt roads in your area. For safety, tell someone where you are going, carry your phone with you, and bring plenty of water.

Workout 3

Objective: Think of this technical workout as a warm-up for workout 7, which focuses on tip contact and resistance.

Time	60 minutes
Terrain	Flat, paved surface
Pace	Moderate
Intensity	65 to 75 percent HRmax
RPE	4 to 5

Fitness Focus: This workout focuses on arm extension, leg extension, and spine rotation. The diverse musculature surrounding the shoulders allows the joints to move the arms in variety of directions and planes. Look at this drill as an exercise in dynamic flexibility that enhances the range of motion and physical capabilities of both your shoulders and your spine.

Comments: To extend your arms farther, imagine an open eyeball in the crease of each elbow. As you walk, never flex your elbows enough to close the eyes! Gentle inclines are ideal for practicing this drill.

Workout 4

Objective: This workout mildly increases heart rate and highlights technique for walking downhill. Your task is to walk downhill with a smooth gait.

Time	60 minutes
Terrain	Flat, dirt surface with moderate incline
Pace	Moderate
Intensity	65 to 75 percent HRmax
RPE	4 to 5

Fitness Focus: Concentrate on building strength in your upper legs. Although you work many of the same muscles whether you go uphill or downhill, they work in different capacities. For example, when walking downhill, a cushioning effort takes place in your lower body. As your heel strikes and the pelvis travels over the leg, your corresponding knee and hip soften. The quadriceps are particularly responsive, producing a negative contraction that lengthens the muscle fibers.

Comments: Regardless of your walking style, make sure to fully engage your feet by rolling from heel to toes.

Workout 5

Objective: In this steady-state workout, decrease stride length to give your lower back and groin a break and work on speed technique.

Time	60 minutes
Terrain	Flat, paved surface
Pace	Moderate
Intensity	70 to 77 percent HRmax
RPE	5 to 6

Fitness Focus: Practice your speed technique (chapter 4). You may not necessarily feel an increase in your heart rate at first, but you should feel an increase in your forward momentum. Long levers, faster arm movements, and a shorter stride length will make your tip contact efficient, which elevates your heart rate.

Comments: Subsequent chapters use speed technique for interval training. Use a shorter stride with a long arm that swings half the distance fore and aft. This strategy works well if you want to continue Nordic walking techniques on steep descents.

Workout 6

Objective: Simply walk without pressuring or rushing yourself. You may find it interesting to wear a heart rate monitor and observe how your body reacts to different terrain.

Time	75 minutes
Terrain	Flat, dirt surface
Pace	Moderate
Intensity	70 to 75 percent HRmax
RPE	5

Fitness Focus: This workout is dedicated to simplicity. This is like a "time out" workout to focus inward. Don't work on anything other than paying attention to how you feel internally.

Comments: Since this is a steady-state workout, use this time to make physical assessments. For example, play with eating different kinds of food prior to the workout. How do you feel halfway through your workout after eating a bowl of oatmeal with milk as compared to yogurt and whole-wheat toast? Is there a difference in your heart rate?

Workout 7

Objective: This workout is where skills meet strength—hills and varied terrain give you the opportunity to practice the techniques of long arms and tip engagement. These skills go hand in hand because your lengthened arm initiates a low-impact relationship between the tip of the pole and the walking surface. Capitalizing on this contact creates resistance for the upper back to get stronger.

Time	75 minutes
Terrain	Paved, rolling hills
Pace	Moderate
Intensity	65 to 77 percent HRmax
RPE	4 to 6

Fitness Focus: Concentrate on strengthening your back by adding resistance when the poles connect with the ground.

Comments: Walk for 15 minutes on flat surfaces at both the beginning and the end of the workout. The beauty of this workout is in natural intervals. Instead of gripping the handle and bearing down on or slapping the terrain, think about receiving the earth with skilled upper-body movements that gently nail the sweet spot of the tips every time. Next, cup the handle firmly and press through the tips. Concentrate on feeling your back muscles work.

Workout 8

Objective: Pay attention to your heart rate as you do the informal distance intervals.

Time	60 minutes
Terrain	Flat, dirt surface
Pace	Moderate but faster
Intensity	70 to 80 percent HRmax
RPE	5 to 7

Fitness Focus: Play with your cadence to increase your heart rate. You should feel your cadence speed up when you move with more forward momentum. During the informal intervals, take several strides to quicken your cadence. Increasing your speed and the resistance created through the tips should raise your heart rate slightly.

Comments: Use a heart rate monitor to take the mystery out of cardio training. Stay in the middle of your heart-rate zone, around 75 percent, for the majority of the workout. Use informal intervals to play with your heart rate by walking quickly to landmarks that are a comfortable distance away.

CHAPTER 10

Medium and Quick

These workouts are a bit more serious and are intended for those who don't like to waste any time. Get right down to business as you train to develop pace, speed, and cardiorespiratory fitness. Some workouts use the speed techniques from chapter 4 and others use interval training. The aerobic activity is an obvious benefit of these workouts. Since you have already experienced Nordic walking, this chapter safely takes your skills to the next level of speed and efficiency.

As in chapters 8 and 9, these workouts help you continue to work on your technique. Regardless of how good you are, you can always learn something new about Nordic walking. This chapter helps you find your ideal pace with enhanced techniques that involve arm movement, stride length, and tip pressure. Interval training pushes your cardiorespiratory limits to both improve and maintain fitness.

The average speed for these workouts is 4 miles (6.4 km) per hour. If you are not used to walking 4 mph, work up to it on a treadmill. This kind of conditioning trains your body to move more quickly and encourages you to work harder. Workouts last 50 to 75 minutes and keep the RPE in the range of 4 to 8. Heart rates are also higher, fluctuating between 65 and 85 percent of the maximum.

You've already experienced how fun it is to walk on dirt. Chapter 10 gives you the opportunity to walk in sand. Sand walking is more challenging because your feet sink, affecting the rhythm and timing of your movements. These short workouts are ideal for the quicker, shorter pace required to walk in sand. Of course, it's also fun to experiment with stride length, plyometrics, and high-intensity activities. However, deep sand combined with a long stride quickly results in anaerobic activity. If your objective is steady-state cardio, you should shorten stride length when walking in sand.

The objective of this chapter is to increase cardiorespiratory capacity and walking speed at a comfortable, safe, and progressive pace. These workouts use a variety of ground surfaces, such as the rolling hills in workout 7. If you can't find rolling hills or inclines in your area, see chapter 14 for challenging workouts that involve open spaces, stairs, and metronomes.

Preview: Medium and Quick Workouts

Workout	Walking time (min)	Terrain	Pace	Intensity (% HRmax / RPE)
1	50	Flat/paved	Moderate	65-70 / 4-5
2	50	Flat/dirt	Moderate	65-70 / 4-5
3	60	Flat/paved/inclines	Moderate	65-80 / 4-7
4	60	Flat/sand	Moderate	65-80 / 4-7
5	60	Flat/paved	Moderate	70-80 / 5-7
6	75	Flat/dirt	Moderate	77-85 / 6-8
7	75	Flat/paved/rolling hills	Moderate	70-85 / 5-8
8	60	Flat/dirt/moderate incline	Moderate/fast	70-85 / 5-8

Workout 1

Objective: Combining awareness of posture with Nordic walking creates core strength, truly making this a full-body workout. Focus on posture as you safely increase your speed. Your movements should be flowing, not stiff or sticklike. Your heart rate should be constant and comfortable.

Time	50 minutes
Terrain	Flat, paved surface
Pace	Moderate
Intensity	65 to 70 percent HRmax
RPE	4 to 5

Fitness Focus: Balance the weight of your head so as not to tax the lower back. Over time, you can feel strain in the lower back when your head has moved away from the ideal position over your pelvis. Walk with upright posture at slow speeds. When you move quickly, it becomes more appropriate to move your head and shoulders forward.

Comments: Review the postural techniques outlined in chapter 3. Remember that the general catalyst for poor posture is the tendency to look down at the ground. Think about holding your chin level with the ground rather than lifting your head up. This practice situates the head over the shoulders and the shoulders over the pelvis, aligning the heaviest parts of your body for a healthy back!

Workout 2

Objective: This steady-state workout takes you over a variety of surfaces, including dirt, grass, and gravel. Focus on balance as the varied terrain gives you a welcome reprieve from hard training.

Time	50 minutes
Terrain	Flat, dirt surface
Pace	Moderate
Intensity	65 to 70 percent HRmax
RPE	4 to 5

Fitness Focus: Draw your awareness to your feet and ankles to improve balance, coordination, and agility. As your lower legs react with small, unplanned movements to the demands of varied terrain, you build your body's balance memory.

Comments: After walking for 10 minutes, look for surface diversions, such as dirt, grass, gravel, sand, or any other surface that presents small challenges to balance. Our favorite is an old, rundown parking lot with cracks in the uneven pavement.

Workout 3

Objective: Hills and intervals of double and single poling (chapter 4) will make your heart rate fluctuate and will engage the muscles of the back.

Time	60 minutes
Terrain	Flat, paved surface with a moderate to steep incline
Pace	Moderate
Intensity	65 to 80 percent HRmax
RPE	4 to 7

Fitness Focus: Walk for 10 minutes at a brisk pace. Over the next 40 minutes, incorporate intervals of different pole work. Perform two two-minute intervals of double poling. Rest between the two intervals by doing three to five minutes of easier walking. Then begin two-minute intervals of single-side poling. For added intensity, do some of the intervals while going uphill.

Comments: Establish a solid connection with your pole tips. The moment you feel the tip making contact, apply pressure until it's time to swing that arm forward again. The longer the poles connect with the walking surface, the stronger your upper body will be.

Workout 4

Objective: Walking in sand is always a reliable cardio workout because the weight of sand creates resistance around your shoes and poles, and you sink as you step. Because you are temporarily less efficient than usual, you work harder to compensate, toughening up the lower legs with small anaerobic movements of the feet and ankles. Refer to the speed technique in chapter 4.

Time	60 minutes
Terrain	Flat, sand surface
Pace	Moderate
Intensity	65 to 80 percent HRmax
RPE	4 to 7

Fitness Focus: Work on moving faster by hustling toward landmarks during intervals. Your stride should be short and your arm swing should be powerful and quick. Focus on stabilizing your ankles and knees to prevent injury. Use this workout as an opportunity to move your ankles through different ranges of motion.

Comments: Walk for 10 minutes to reach the middle of your heart rate zone, and then begin sand spurts! Alternate three-minute spurts with six minutes of active rest. Complete this process four times.

Workout 5

Objective: Now it's time to walk with and without poles. Many people report that they walk much stronger without poles after Nordic walking; the body continues to mimic the postures of Nordic walking. This phenomenon, called kinesthetic aftereffect, lasts only seconds or minutes.

Time	60 minutes
Terrain	Flat, paved surface
Pace	Moderate
Intensity	70 to 80 percent HRmax
RPE	5 to 7

Fitness Focus: Focus awareness on your body as you alternate between intervals using poles and walking without them. Think about your upper back. Can you feel a difference? Is it also more difficult to sustain forward momentum without poles? Try to maintain the same pace during the segment without poles.

Comments: Do six segments of 10 minutes each and walk three segments with poles and three without. When you aren't using the poles for walking, hold them in the middle with the handles pointing forward. Try to keep them level with the ground while power walking.

Workout 6

Objective: Walking to the constant beat of a metronome creates the perfect workout for burning fat and calories! Experiment with different speeds until you find a beat that feels aggressive but does not compromise your technique.

Time	75 minutes
Terrain	Flat, dirt surface
Pace	Moderate
Intensity	77 to 85 percent HRmax
RPE	6 to 8

Fitness Focus: Focus on how your pelvis reacts to tip pressure and subsequent spine rotation to move in the opposite direction, try to feel all your core muscles engaging. As you increase the pace, try to maintain intensity in the upper body.

Comments: After walking for 10 minutes, turn on the metronome and walk to the beat until you reach 80 percent of your training heart rate (90-120 bpm). Walk at this level for 20 minutes, and then concentrate on applying tip pressure for two minutes. Increase your walking speed with the help of the metronome to reach 85 percent. Use the last 20 minutes to gradually decrease intensity back to 77 percent.

Medium and Quick

Workout 7

Objective: Some people have a difficult time mastering the handle release. It can feel unnatural, expecially if stride length is not developed. Assume a constant pace on a flat surface to work on the passive release from chapter 3, which involves opening your hand as it passes your hip.

Time	75 minutes
Terrain	Flat, paved surface with rolling hills
Pace	Moderate
Intensity	70 to 85 percent HRmax
RPE	5 to 8

Fitness Focus: Just after tip contact is complete, relax the muscles in the back, shoulder, arm, and then the hand during the release. Assuming a longer stride length or bounding (chapter 4) will give you more time to effectively release the handle. Cup it with intention on the way back.

Comments: Keep your wrists neutral as they travel behind your body; don't flex, twist, or rotate your hands or arms. Shoulder injuries occur when joints are taken through the full range of motion while carrying a load!

Workout 8

Objective: Use a monitor for this workout, which features a combination of steady-state work and either speed walking or running (chapter 4). It is ideal if you are training for endurance. Your heart rate varies with the terrain. Add intensity with interval work and hills.

Time	60 minutes
Terrain	Flat, dirt surface with moderate incline
Pace	Moderate to fast
Intensity	70 to 85 percent HRmax
RPE	5 to 8

Fitness Focus: Pay attention to your heart rate and adjust your stride to stay in your target zone. Monitor how much your heart rate lowers on the walk downhill. If it drops too much (to an RPE of 2 or 3), pick up your pace but shorten your stride length.

Comments: Program your minimum and maximum heart rates into your monitor. Spend 10 minutes working up to pace, and then add a two-minute interval of high-intensity activity every seven minutes or so. Continue this process for the next 45 minutes. Stay above your minimum heart rate during recovery walking and just below your maximum heart rate during the intervals.

CHAPTER **11**

Short and Fast

Once you have developed significant endurance and have refined your technique to establish a baseline of fitness, you can focus primarily on speed and strength. This concept, which is initially presented in the workouts of the previous chapter, is expanded and enhanced in this chapter. After gradually training for aerobic endurance, you should be physically prepared to handle short and fast workouts. By now, you can also benefit psychologically from a distinct and fun change in pace.

These demanding workouts are intended for intermediate or advanced Nordic walkers, and should only be performed once or twice a week. Short and fast workouts involve a different bodily system for metabolizing energy. During these bouts, the working muscles cannot access very much oxygen and must use energy that is available in very small quantities. You must schedule recovery time in order to perform consecutive workouts and to minimize the risk of injuries and infections of the upper respiratory tract.

These workouts are very convenient if you are short on time. The high intensity offsets the need for a long workout. Keep in mind that the times listed for the following workouts do not include warm-up and cool-down periods. Because these workouts are so high in intensity, gradual warm-ups are essential for making the muscles and soft tissue more pliable and resilient. You must also cool-down gradually after the workout so that your body can flush waste products out of the muscles that may otherwise lead to tightness and soreness.

The following workouts are listed in order of increasing difficulty, as measured by distance, time, and intensity. They range in RPE from 5 to 8 and last 25 to 40 minutes. They also incorporate inclines, which are a great way to work various muscle groups. Much like adding weights on a barbell to increase the load, introducing inclined terrain makes the workout more challenging, since the gravity acts like extra weight. As discussed in chapter 3, you can also increase tip pressure to make the workout more challenging.

This chapter introduces the concept of timed speed intervals, which are a fantastic tool for increasing intensity. Intervals are mostly performed on flat surfaces, although a hilly terrain can also serve as a natural interval course. Be careful not to injure yourself when introducing speed intervals on an incline. Because of the high intensity of interval training, you must limit this type of workout to a few days a week.

Preview: Short and Fast Workouts

Workout	Distance (mi / km)	Walking time (min)	Terrain	Pace	Intensity (% HRmax/RPE)
1	1.25/2	25	Flat/some inclines	Easy/moderate	75-79/5-6
2	1.5/2.4	25	Flat/paved	Moderate	75-79/5-6
3	2/3.2	25	Flat/dirt	Fast	80-84/6-7
4	2/3.2	30	Flat/some inclines	Moderate	80-84/6-7
5	2.5/4	30	Flat/paved	Fast	80-84/6-7
6	2.5/4	35	Flat/some inclines	Moderate	85-89/7-8
7	3/5	35	Flat/paved	Fast	85-89/7-8
8	3/5	40	Flat/some inclines	Fast	85-89/7-8

Workout 1

Objective: This short and fast workout sets the stage for more challenging workouts in the future.

Distance	1.25 miles (2 km)
Time	25 minutes
Terrain	Flat surface with some inclines
Pace	Easy to moderate
Intensity	75 to 79 percent HRmax
RPE	5 to 6

Fitness Focus: After warming up for five minutes, establish a good rhythm, and then increase the intensity a bit by walking up a low-grade incline.

Comments: Your pace should be comfortable throughout. Incorporate a few bouts of harder work into the routine and finish with a cool-down on flat terrain.

Workout 2

Objective: Although the distance of this short and sweet workout is slightly longer than the last one was, aim to finish with the same time.

Distance	1.5 miles (2.4 km)
Time	25 minutes
Terrain	Flat, paved surface
Pace	Moderate
Intensity	75 to 79 percent HRmax
RPE	5 to 6

Fitness Focus: After your warm-up, perform 5 intervals of 10 seconds each with an active rest period of 30 seconds in between. If this is not challenging enough, shorten the active rest time. During the active rest periods, you should be walking at your normal pace. Because these high-intensity workouts offer a great cardiorespiratory challenge, be sure to cool down for at least five minutes at the end.

Comments: Since there are no hills, get into a great rhythm and then concentrate on form for the full routine.

Short and Fast

Workout 3

Objective: This routine ramps up the distance and intensity. Focus on maintaining your form at a faster and more progressive pace.

Distance	2 miles (3.2 km)
Time	25 minutes
Terrain	Flat, dirt surface
Pace	Fast
Intensity	80 to 84 percent HRmax
RPE	6 to 7

Fitness Focus: Choosing a dirt path can make this walk more fun. Be sure to apply adequate pressure to the pole tips to keep up the pace as you move forward. After warm-up, perform three intervals lasting 20 to 30 seconds. Be sure to actively rest for at least two minutes in between.

Comments: You can do this shorter workout when you don't have much time to exercise. The intensity of the routine makes up for its brevity. If the intervals are too intense to start, lengthen the active rest period to allow for recovery before doing another.

Workout 4

Objective: Work on both form and speed as you tackle some inclines.

Distance	2 miles (3.2 km)
Time	30 minutes
Terrain	Flat surface with some inclines
Pace	Moderate
Intensity	80 to 84 percent HRmax
RPE	6 to 7

Fitness Focus: Try to walk the second half just as quickly as you did the first.

Comments: Find a route that takes you up and down a hill at least once to elevate your heart rate. You can lower the pace a bit during the inclines in order to handle them with impeccable form. The inclines become your natural, built-in intervals.

Short and Fast

Workout 5

Objective: This moderate workout prepares you for the next one, which is more intense.

Distance	2.5 miles (4 km)
Time	30 minutes
Terrain	Flat, paved surface
Pace	Fast
Intensity	80 to 84 percent HRmax
RPE	6 to 7

Fitness Focus: As you focus on distance and speed, make your leg and arm movements as fluid as possible. This practice will make your stride more efficient and will help you finish strong. After warm-up, perform four intervals lasting 20 to 30 seconds, with active rest periods at least three times as long (60-90 seconds).

Comments: Choose a flat asphalt surface to help you move efficiently and quickly.

Workout 6

Objective: This workout ramps up the distance. Pick a route that takes you up and down moderate hills several times.

Distance	2.5 miles (4 km)
Time	35 minutes
Terrain	Flat surface with some inclines
Pace	Moderate
Intensity	85 to 89 percent HRmax
RPE	7 to 8

Fitness Focus: These intervals challenge your cardiorespiratory system by forcing it to work hard. Concentrate on recovering immediately after the more difficult passes.

Comments: Since this workout challenges the upper limits of your heart rate, cool down and stretch afterwards.

Workout 7

Objective: The distance and speed of this workout are greater than any in this series so far. In this situation, quick and steady wins the race, so move as fast as you can.

Distance	3 miles (5 km)
Time	35 minutes
Terrain	Flat, paved surface
Pace	Fast
Intensity	85 to 89 percent HRmax
RPE	7 to 8

Fitness Focus: The more efficient your stride and upper-body movements are, the farther you will go. Focus on maintaining strong, upright posture and long limbs. After warm-up, perform five intervals lasting 40 to 60 seconds. Be sure to actively rest for at least two minutes in between. If this is not challenging enough, shorten the rest period to one minute.

Comments: Do not compromise technique for speed in this workout. Try to do both with a strong gliding finish.

Workout 8

Objective: The challenge here is to combine distance, speed, and precise form on the inclines.

Distance	3 miles (5 km)
Time	40 minutes
Terrain	Flat surface with some inclines
Pace	Fast
Intensity	85 to 89 percent HRmax
RPE	7 to 8

Fitness Focus: Focus on technique to move up the hills, maintaining great posture as you push off the ground from behind. Use the poles to engage the upper body and lessen the load on the legs.

Comments: At this point, it is not acceptable to have sloppy technique on the hills. Even if you are tired, you have put too much work into developing precise form to give up now! As you go up and down the hills, relax your upper body, particularly the shoulders and neck. Every step should be fluid.

CHAPTER 12

Long and Steady

They say that slow and steady wins the race. Whether you are training for an endurance event, such as a 10K or half marathon, or are increasing your distance to burn more calories, workouts that are long and steady can make you a winner as well.

The previous chapter enhances anaerobic energy, which trains the body to handle quick, intense bursts of effort. Anaerobic training comes in handy when you attempt longer distances, particularly if you wish to go faster as well. It also helps your body tolerate high-intensity by-products of exercise, such as lactic acid. Therefore, you will be able to perform at a higher intensity for longer durations without fatigue.

The following workouts utilize the aerobic system to fully derive energy from the activity. You can select workouts based on the amount of time you have for exercise, or on a specific distance if you are training for a long event. As in the previous chapter, you should only perform long workouts once or twice a week. You must vary the intensity of weekly workouts in order to keep your body and mind fresh. The workouts in this chapter range in RPE from 5 to 8. If your body does not have adequate time to recover, you put yourself at risk of overtraining and injury. For example, performing long-distance, high-intensity workouts back to back can both exhaust your body and suppress your immune response. In order to give 100 percent on every workout and to minimize infection of the upper respiratory tract, you must follow high-intensity routines with low- or moderate-intensity routines. Chapter 17 discusses the philosophy of periodization in greater detail.

The total walking times in the following workouts do not include times for warming up and cooling down. Therefore, considering that the total exercise time ranges from 70 to 210 minutes, you must properly hydrate and fuel your body. The body releases and relieves the excess heat generated by exercise through respiration, convection, perspiration, and evaporation. You must drink fluids during intense or long bouts of exercise in order to replenish these lost fluids and to assist your organs and working muscles in regulating internal temperature. Although it should go without saying, wear proper gear to protect yourself from the elements as well.

Preview: Long and Steady Workouts

Workout	Distance (mi/km)	Walking time (min)	Terrain	Pace	Intensity (% HRmax/RPE)
1	3.5/5.6	60	Flat/slight inclines	Moderate	75-84/5-6
2	4.5/7.2	77	Flat/paved	Moderate	75-79/5
3	6/10	90	Flat/slight inclines	Moderate	75-84/5-6
4	7.5/12	100	Flat/paved	Fast	80-84/6
5	9/14.5	120	Flat/paved	Fast	80-84/6
6	10.5/17	157	Flat/slight inclines	Moderate	75-89/5-7
7	12/19	180	Flat/slight inclines	Moderate	75-89/5-7
8	15/24	200	Flat/paved	Fast	80-89/6-8

Workout 1

Objective: This is a great workout for testing your endurance.

Distance	3.5 miles (5.6 km)
Time	60 minutes
Terrain	Flat surface with slight inclines
Pace	Moderate
Intensity	75 to 84 percent HRmax
RPE	5 to 6

Fitness Focus: Although the terrain should be predominantly flat, try to challenge yourself with some slight inclines in the middle of the routine.

Comments: Begin with a gradual warm-up, settle into a comfortable pace, and attempt to maintain the pace during the inclines. Be sure to bring some water, since you will be exercising for an hour.

Workout 2

Objective: This workout builds distance. The consistently moderate pace takes you over flat terrain.

Distance	4.5 miles (7.2 km)
Time	77 minutes
Terrain	Flat, paved surface
Pace	Moderate
Intensity	75 to 79 percent HRmax
RPE	5

Fitness Focus: The consistent terrain gives you an opportunity to demonstrate great technique throughout the whole workout.

Comments: Warm up gradually, and then get into a groove to walk the duration without modifying your pace. Find a path where you can enjoy the scenery once you've established your rhythm. Since the workout is longer than 60 minutes, be sure to bring an electrolyte drink along.

Long and Steady

Workout 3

Objective: Finishing this workout at a moderate pace is a great accomplishment, given the distance and added inclines.

Distance	6 miles (10 km)
Time	90 minutes
Terrain	Flat surface with slight inclines
Pace	Moderate
Intensity	75 to 84 percent HRmax
RPE	5 to 6

Fitness Focus: To challenge your heart and vary the workout, push through a few slight inclines without slowing down.

Comments: As in the previous workout, finding a rhythm will help you go the distance. Maintain strict form when going up and down inclines.

Workout 4

Objective: Revel in the accomplishment of walking more than 7 miles!

Distance	7.5 miles (12 km)
Time	100 minutes
Terrain	Flat, paved surface
Pace	Fast
Intensity	80 to 84 percent HRmax
RPE	6

Fitness Focus: Try to avoid feeling breathless as you increase your speed. Instead, enjoy a pace that makes you feel as if you are on a moving side-walk. Focus on keeping your stride length and arm swing long to maintain momentum.

Comments: The pace should be fast during this routine. Remember the technique you learned in the speed and interval workouts.

Workout 5

Objective: Although the distance and time are slightly greater, your speed should be similar to the one you established in the previous workout.

Distance	9 miles (14.5 km)
Time	120 minutes
Terrain	Flat, paved surface
Pace	Fast
Intensity	80 to 84 percent HRmax
RPE	6

Fitness Focus: Check your breathing every 10 minutes. Even when walking at a fast pace, you should not feel out of breath.

Comments: Once you have completed 7 miles, 9 miles should be no sweat. Again, moderate your intensity to ensure that you cross the finish line. Consider doing this routine with another Nordic walker to pass the time easily.

Workout 6

Objective: The overall pace should be moderate; this is not a workout for speed.

Distance	10.5 miles (17 km)
Time	157 minutes
Terrain	Flat surface with slight inclines
Pace	Moderate
Intensity	75 to 89 percent HRmax
RPE	5 to 7

Fitness Focus: Use the rubber tips to push off the ground and to propel you farther with each step, particularly when going up mild inclines.

Comments: The distance and inclines of this workout will raise your heart rate for short stints and will push you to your upper limits. Make sure you bring an electrolyte-replacement drink or some carbohydrate snacks to help your body maintain intensity.

Long and Steady

Workout 7

Objective: Again, the pace is moderate to ensure that you can complete the distance. Try a few inclines to really test your endurance and power.

Distance	12 miles (19 km)
Time	180 minutes
Terrain	Flat surface with slight inclines
Pace	Moderate
Intensity	75 to 89 percent HRmax
RPE	5 to 7

Fitness Focus: Since it is only temporary, embrace the breathlessness you may feel going up the inclines. Breathe in a rhythmic pattern where you inhale for two steps, then exhale for two steps to keep the right amount of oxygen entering your system to keep you going strong.

Comments: Once you have gone 12 miles, a distance of 15 (24 km) is right around the corner. Engage your upper body a bit more on the inclines to preserve the effort of your legs for long strides at the finish.

Workout 8

Objective: The pace should be fast yet controlled to accomplish 15 miles. You are surpassing the distance of a half marathon!

Distance	15 miles (24 km)
Time	200 minutes
Terrain	Flat, paved surface
Pace	Fast
Intensity	80 to 89 percent HRmax
RPE	6 to 8

Fitness Focus: Focus on the basic fundamentals to efficiently finish the walk. Periodically monitor your stride length, trunk rotation, arm swing, and contact of the pole with the ground.

Comments: You must call upon the successes of the previous workouts to give you the confidence to keep going. Feel the poles propelling you forward. Remember that you have trained to do this. You must bring sources of hydration and food to help you go the distance. Indulge in the feeling of success once you have finished this workout. Is a marathon in your future?

CHAPTER **13**

Outdoor Circuit Training

Exercising in nature is an expression of physical freedom that inspires motivation. It's tough to find a better gym than the outdoors—the space is free of walls, equipment, sign-up sheets, and crowds. Furthermore, these unique and fun total-body workouts are completely free.

Circuit training is typically a total-body workout in which you perform a series of different tasks, drills, and exercises, alternating intervals of cardio with drills for strength, agility, and power. Beyond the cardiovascular benefits, you will also improve your posture, balance, strength, flexibility, lean muscle mass, and responses of the nervous system.

In classic circuit training, you rest very little between exercises. This practice promotes cardiovascular conditioning and caloric burn, keeps your heart rate elevated, and raises resting metabolism. Therefore, you can do more work in less time. However, this chapter builds in times of active rest. If you do not feel like resting, do another set!

Please review the information from chapter 4 on preventing injuries before performing plyometrics and other high-impact drills. It isn't healthy to drastically change your stride length or intensity level overnight. Certain drills in this chapter, such as agility training and forward bounding, require you to quickly adjust your stride length, sometimes even while in the air. View the workouts below with an eye for outdoor safety, paying attention to what feels right for your body. As training grows more intense, injuries related to overuse become more prevalent. Therefore, this chapter takes great care to introduce programs, workouts, and recommendations for exercises in logical progressions so that your body can safely adapt to the new experiences.

In the 1980s, I created Outdoor Cross-Training, a fitness program that draws inspiration from the natural environment for equipment and workouts. Back then, we practiced balance on sidewalk curbs and agility on sidewalk lines. This chapter has updated the programs to include poles, trees, stairs, hills, and more. Parks and playgrounds are excellent spaces for this type of circuit workout.

This chapter outlines three kinds of outdoor workouts for supporting your athletic goals and conditioning your body. Terrain for these workouts is varied. All you need to perform freestyle workouts is a walking path. For boot-camp workouts, you'll need access to an open area such as a soccer field or a park. During freestyle workouts, be creative with the outdoor terrain. You might create intervals of running or fast walking toward a chosen object. Make choices of different distances and modify your pace to match the distance. If you're with a group, take turns choosing.

Four freestyle and boot-camp workouts blend intervals of Nordic walking intervals with different kinds of movement. Some are slow and calculated, while others are cardiovascular in nature, such as agility training, running, or plyometrics. Fartlek, or speed play, is variable-pace running or fast walking that emphasizes creativity.

- *Freestyle 1 and 2*. These workouts are environmental fitness at its best! The corresponding section gives you tools for assessing your outdoor walking terrain. Each workout has recommendations for certain types of exercises and drills, but you are also free to come up with your own version.

- *Boot camp 1 and 2*. These traditional sports-conditioning workouts are regimented and presented step by step, so you won't miss a beat.

- *Flow 1, 2, and 3*. These workouts are holistic with an internal focus on the aesthetics of body awareness and movement. They are intended for days of active recovery and do not include a classic circuit-training component. Instead, they include tasks for you to perform, such as drills that improve walking posture or balance in motion. Body-focus drills create the flow experience, or the physical relationships among the walker, the poles, the path, and everything else associated with exercising outside.

Chapters 4 and 5 outline the exercises and drills referenced in this chapter. Partner drills add an element of resistance and fun that is difficult to reproduce indoors. For example, during flow workouts, you can try to synchronize your walking, following the pace, timing, and cadence of a friend.

These workouts last between 30 to 90 minutes, including warm-up and cool-down. Intensity is built progressively. Balance, agility, and power tasks are timed and based on your own perception of effort. Set your own pace and march to a beat that works for you.

Components of a Safe Workout

Before venturing out, review the guidelines for outdoor safety in chapter 6. Be aware of your own personal space and that of your walking partners. Limit your movements to those that feel safe. If you don't care for an exercise, don't choose it. Chapter 4 presents ample exercises and drills for creating a well-rounded workout. All of the workouts in this chapter adhere to the following basic template.

• *Warm-up.* Warm up for 10 minutes before starting the bulk of your workout. If you plan to work out for longer than the guidelines dictate, extend your warm-up time as well.

• *Cardiovascular segment.* You'll spend 25 to 60 minutes on this section. Cardiovascular activity is not always steady-state work. Mix longer intervals of cardio with other tasks to enhance dynamic balance, coordination, strength, agility, and power. You can do intervals and repetition as prescribed by the guidelines of your workout or as a spontaneous reaction to your environment. Freestyle workouts let you take advantage of the impulses of the moment.

• *Strength segment(s).* Strength training is mixed into all workouts, with the exception of flow routines, in intervals that are either timed or repeated. Some are performed while standing and others while moving. Dynamic-strength exercises, which involve pole resistance, are performed on the fly. For skill development workouts, do a set that has 8 to 12 reps of 8 to 10 exercises. Perform this set twice weekly. You should be able to complete the workout in 20 minutes. For fitness proficiency workouts do two sets two times a week for 30 minutes. Each set contains 10 to 12 reps of 8 to 10 exercises. Finally, for competition workouts, do two or three sets (10 to 15 reps of 8 to 10 exercises) twice weekly. Each set should last about 45 minutes.

• *Stability training.* Work on stationary balance either at the beginning or end of your workout. Research shows that balance recovery is more challenging when fatigue has already set in. Play with this concept during your workouts and remember that the goal of balance training is not to control your body. Rather, work to accept the feeling of being out of control, especially at the ankles and feet! The advanced tasks of dynamic balance and coordination take place while you are moving. The flexibility exercises enhance range of motion by extending your limbs.

• *Cool-down.* Walk at an easy pace for four minutes or longer.

• *Flexibility.* Stretch for at least four minutes (see chapter 5 for more details). Keep things simple so you can relish the last minutes of your time outside.

Outdoor Circuits: Assess Your Terrain

These circuit workouts require appropriate outdoor terrain. Open soccer fields and large parks work well for boot-camp workouts. Many of the exercises and tasks require grassy fields. The sole requirement for flow workouts is a walking path, since the aim of these routines is to meditate as you walk.

Other than your fitness level and training goals, the only limit to the tasks you can try is your imagination. Your choice of terrain depends on the safe outdoor spaces in your area and your own personal preferences. Choose your terrain with the following activities in mind:

- *Intervals of Nordic walking, jogging, and running.* These tasks, such as using hills to increase intensity, utilize various speeds, inclines, and surfaces.
- *Balance.* These tasks, such as standing on one foot on a low wall, usually involve balancing on a stable object.
- *Dynamic balance.* These tasks, such as walking over a downed log, usually require directional movement. Try to balance on an unstable object with one or both legs.
- *Strength.* These tasks, which include pushing, pulling, squatting, and lifting exercises, can be adapted for your environment.
- *Speed work.* These tasks, which involve a faster pace, are easy to facilitate but more difficult in terms of intensity. For example, pick a landmark ahead and Nordic walk toward it as fast as you can.
- *Plyometrics.* This type of explosive power training is characterized by repeated loading and unloading of muscles. Exercises include hopping, skipping, jumping, bounding, and leaping. Try bounding forward using your poles as props.
- *Agility.* These tasks require fast footwork to maintain your balance as you change directions quickly. Drills include starting, stopping, and pivoting suddenly.
- *Coordination.* Try to connect the movements of your upper and lower body. Tasks include throwing an object in the air and kicking it, or a double pole toss.

Freestyle Workouts

Freestyle workouts can be developed for any outdoor environment. For example, creatively plan exercises and tasks for the structures and features of a school playground with large open spaces. Freestyle workouts let you add other components of conditioning to typically cardiovascular workouts.

Freestyle 1

Time	60 minutes
Pace	Easy and moderate
Intensity	65 to 75 percent HRmax
RPE	4 to 7

Warm-Up: Walk at an easy pace for 10 minutes.

Walk: Spend 25 minutes on this segment. Walk at your fitness pace to reach your target heart rate. This workout does not include power training.

- *Dynamic strength 1.* Perform single-side poling for the last four minutes of your walk. Use the pole for two minutes on each side.

Strength: This segment should last six minutes (five minutes of activity and one minute of total rest). Select three strength exercises from chapter 4: one for the lower body, one for the core, and one for upper body. Perform one or two sets of each exercise according to your fitness level. Rest for 30 seconds between sets.

- *Strength 1.* Lower body: Do stationary squats.
- *Strength 2.* Core: Raise opposing arms and legs from a stationary position or perform single-side poling.
- *Strength 3.* Upper body: Do classic push-ups or a front press with a partner.

Agility: Spend five minutes on this segment. Select two agility tasks from chapter 5 and perform each task twice. Nordic walk for two minutes between intervals.

- *Agility 1.* Do a crossover walk.
- *Agility 2.* Perform step-ups on a curb.

Dynamic Flexibility: Spend three minutes on this segment. Select two dynamic flexibility exercises from chapter 5. Perform one or two consecutive sets. Do active walking for two minutes between sets.

- *Dynamic flexibility 1.* Perform knee lifts.
- *Dynamic flexibility 2.* Perform backside kickers.

Cool-Down: Walk at an easy pace for five minutes.

Balance and Coordination: Spend one minute on this segment. Select one stationary balance task from chapter 5.

Flexibility: Spend five minutes doing stretches from chapter 5.

Outdoor Circuit Training

Freestyle 2

Time	75 minutes
Pace	Moderate and more difficult
Intensity	65 to 94 percent HRmax
RPE	5 to 9

Warm-Up: Walk at an easy pace for 10 minutes.

Walk: Spend 30 minutes on this segment. Add speed technique for the first 10 minutes. During the next 20 minutes, add three two-minute speed intervals. Walk at a normal pace for four minutes between intervals. This workout adds speed and power. It is a lunger's dream and an author favorite.

Strength: Spend 12 minutes on this segment. Select six strength exercises from chapter 4: two for the lower body, two for the core, and two for the upper body. Perform these exercises as intervals injected into a normal walking routine or do them as a progression.

- *Strength 1.* Lower body: Do stationary lunges.
- *Strength 2.* Lower body: Perform walking lunges.
- *Strength 3.* Upper body: Perform multidirectional arm movements.
- *Strength 4.* Core: Walk or run with both poles.
- *Strength 5.* Upper body: Front press with a partner.
- *Strength 6.* Core: Work on rotation with resistance. Perform this drill with a partner.

Agility: Spend four minutes on this segment. Select two agility tasks from chapter 5. Perform each task for two minutes with little rest in between, or walk for a few minutes before adding them in.

Dynamic Flexibility: Spend four minutes on this segment. Select two exercises for dynamic flexibility. Perform each drill for two minutes.

Power: Spend four minutes on this segment. Select two power tasks from chapter 4 and perform each task twice. Do each drill for one minute and Nordic walk for one minute between drills.

Coordination and Balance: Select one coordination drill and do it for three minutes.

Cool-Down: Walk at an easy pace for four minutes.

Flexibility: Perform four minutes of stretches from chapter 5.

Outdoor Circuit Training

Boot-Camp Workouts

These basic workouts utilize all the tasks, exercises, and drills from chapters 4 and 5. These are more intense and more regimented with formal timed intervals. In order to prevent injuries, you must do functional, traditional strength training for at least three or four weeks before performing plyometrics and power drills. Find an open space like a soccer field for these workouts. You should bring a stopwatch and a workout buddy with you.

Boot Camp 1

Time	60 minutes
Pace	Challenging
Intensity	70 to 80 percent HRmax
RPE	5 to 7

Warm-Up: Spend five minutes performing the warm-up moves previously mentioned, then walk for five more minutes at an easy pace.

Walk: Spend 20 minutes on this segment of straight cardio. Gradually pick up the pace to reach 75 percent of your maximum heart rate. During the last five minutes, do a distance challenge. Pick a landmark in the distance and use speed technique to walk as quickly as possible toward it. Your muscles are now sufficiently warm for more intense drills.

Dynamic Flexibility: Spend four minutes on this segment, allotting two minutes for each drill. Perform these drills consecutively without resting in between.

- *Dynamic flexibility 1.* Do leg lifts to the side.
- *Dynamic flexibility 2.* Perform toe touches that are either stationary or dynamic.

Agility: Spend three minutes on this segment. Perform one minute of each drill without resting in between.

- *Agility 1.* Perform step-ups on a curb.
- *Agility 2.* Slalom through trees.

Power: Spend five minutes on this segment. Perform each power drill for two minutes. Rest for one minute between drills.

- *Power 1.* Perform stationary jumps.
- *Power 2.* Do forward bounding.

(continued)

Outdoor Circuit Training

Boot Camp 1 *(continued)*

Strength: Spend eight minutes on this segment. Perform these strength exercises in the order given with little rest in between.

- *Strength 1.* Lower body: Leverage the lower legs.
- *Strength 2.* Upper body: Perform multidirectional arm raises.
- *Dynamic Strength 3.* Core: Do single-poling exercises while moving forward.
- *Strength 4.* Upper body: Do an underhand row.

Balance and Coordination: Spend two minutes on this segment. You can either mix the drills with tasks that are more intense or perform them as part of your cool-down.

- *Balance and coordination 1.* Perform a single-side balance drill (30 seconds per side).
- *Balance and coordination 2.* Mirror a partner for one minute.

Cool-Down: Spend four minutes walking at an easy pace.

Flexibility: Spend four minutes doing stretches from chapter 5.

Boot Camp 2

Time	90 minutes
Pace	More difficult
Intensity	75 to 94 percent HRmax
RPE	6 to 9

Warm-Up: Spend five minutes performing the warm-up moves previously mentioned, then walk for five more minutes at an easy or moderate pace.

Walk: Spend 35 minutes on this segment. As you walk or run, gradually pick up your pace until you reach 75 percent of your maximum heart rate. Your muscles are now sufficiently warm for more intense drills. Intervals of strength, agility, and power drills are mixed into the routine. Your heart rate will elevate quickly during the high-impact running and plyometric drills. Perform the drills in the given order for a challenging and high-impact workout.

Dynamic Flexibility: Spend six minutes on this segment, allotting two minutes for each drill. Perform these drills consecutively without resting in between.

- *Dynamic flexibility 1.* Perform knee lifts that are either stationary or dynamic.
- *Dynamic flexibility 2.* Perform backside kickers that are either stationary or dynamic.
- *Dynamic flexibility 3.* Perform toe touches that are either stationary or dynamic.

Agility: Spend six minutes on this segment, allotting one minute for each drill. Perform each task twice with little rest in between.

- *Agility 1.* Perform a crossover walk.
- *Agility 2.* Perform a single-side agility drill.
- *Agility 3.* Slalom through trees.

Power: Spend 15 minutes on this segment, allotting two minutes for each drill. Perform each task once, with one minute of Nordic walking between drills. After completing these tasks, walk for another four minutes before beginning strength exercises.

- *Power 1.* Perform stationary jumps.
- *Power 2.* Bound forward, pushing with both poles.
- *Power 3.* Power skip.
- *Power 4.* Perform old-fashioned step-ups with spring in your step.

Strength: Spend eight minutes on this segment, allotting two minutes for each drill. Perform these strength exercises consecutively with little rest in between.

- *Strength 1.* Lower body: Perform single-side squats from a stationary position.
- *Dynamic strength 2.* Lower body: Perform continuous walking lunges.
- *Dynamic strength 3.* Core: Do resistance rotation with partner.
- *Strength 4.* Upper body: Do triceps press.

Balance and Coordination: Perform one of the following drills for two minutes: controlled jousting or mirroring. You can either alternate the drill with more intense tasks or perform it as part of your cool-down.

Cool-Down: Spend four minutes walking at an easy pace.

Flexibility: Perform stretches from chapter 5 for four minutes.

Flow Workouts

These workouts focus on the holistic experience of fitness through Nordic walking. Since they don't include reps, sets, or timed intervals, they are appropriate for rest days. You'll become more aware of your body, which creates healthier movements. Perform body-focus drills on your own time. The rhythmic drills of flow 3 work well with music.

Flow 1: Stress-Reduction Walk

Time	35 minutes
Pace	Easy
Intensity	60 to 70 percent HRmax
RPE	3 to 5

Warm-Up: Walk at an easy pace for 10 minutes.

Cardio: Spend 20 minutes on this segment. Forget about the troubles of your day as you focus on the rhythm of your stride and your breath. This is an easy and relaxing walk for a rest day. Perform two body-focus drills as you walk.

- *Body focus 1.* Crossover walk to trick your body into rotating the spine. Pretend you are on the show *America's Next Top Model!* Pay attention to the feeling of rotation and to the coordinated efforts of your upper and lower body.

- *Body focus 2.* Think of a sentence that depicts the way you'd like to see yourself and repeat it throughout your workout. Positive affirmations work! Mantras include "My body is lean and strong," and "I am happy, healthy, and productive."

Cool-Down: Walk at an easy pace for five minutes and stretch afterwards.

Flow 2: Walking Meditation

Time	60 minutes
Pace	Easy to moderate
Intensity	65 to 75 percent HRmax
RPE	4 to 7

Warm-Up: Warm up for 10 minutes, then gradually increase the intensity to set a steady pace for the entire workout.

Cardio: Spend 45 minutes on this segment. Increase walking pace to match your target heart rate. You don't need to time your body-focus drills. Perform them along the way and tune into your ability to walk efficiently. Pay attention to what is happening within you. Listen to everything about your experience, from the sounds of the birds to your breath. This rest-day workout emphasizes the aesthetic qualities of movements such as breath, posture, and balance. This routine helps you develop better posture, which enhances equilibrium and balance.

- *Body focus 1.* As you walk, pay attention to your body, beginning with the soles of your feet. Pay attention to changes in pressure as you roll from the heel through the toes. Next, watch how your knees react to footwork. Feel the sensation of the legs swinging from the hip sockets like a pendulum. Feel how your torso rotates with each swing of the arms. As the tip of the pole makes contact after the arm swing, focus on the feeling of strength in the upper-body muscles. Focus on keeping your chin level with the walking surface. Finally, be aware of how upright and efficient your posture is! Relax by listening to natural earth sounds and the sound of your breath.

- *Body focus 2.* Perform a stabilization challenge. Look for a curb, low wall or tree to walk along and balance. Balance is best when you focus ahead. If you stop on the log, the longer you stand there, the more chance you are allowing your body to lose balance so keep moving! Keep foot placement precise.

- *Body focus 3.* Remove the pole straps from your wrists. Hold your arms shoulder-width apart at a position no higher than your navel. Imagine that both of your hands and your forehead are corners of an equilateral triangle. Balance the poles horizontally on top of your wrists. Try not to drop them as you walk. Pay attention to any extra movement in your body. For example, don't waddle from side to side or bounce on the balls of your feet.

- *Body focus 4.* Strap the poles back on and imagine a low ceiling over your head that prevents you from bouncing up and down as you walk.

Cool-Down: Take five minutes to cool down and stretch.

Flow 3: Rhythm and Cadence

Time	75 minutes
Pace	Moderate and more difficult
Intensity	70 to 90 percent HRmax
RPE	5 to 9

Warm-Up: During 10 minutes of walking, gradually increase the intensity to reach 75 to 80 percent of your maximum heart rate.

Cardio: Spend 60 minutes on this segment. Increase walking pace and cadence until you reach your target heart rate. Refine your Nordic walking skills with these body-focus drills. You don't need to perform all the drills every time you go out. This workout is very rhythmic, so bring along your music!

- *Body focus 1.* Rhythmic walking is a continuous flow of motion, without stalls or delays. Gripping the handles of your poles loosely, coordinate your breathing with the rhythm of your stride. Pay attention to the timing of your gait and the opposition of your upper and lower body.

- *Body focus 2.* Nordic walking becomes proficient when skill execution is automatic and perfectly timed. Your heel meets the surface at the moment of tip contact, so at the same time. Watch how this drill enhances your timing and cadence, resulting in rhythm.

- *Body focus 3.* Listen to your favorite fast-tempo music and try to match your stride to the beat. If the music is too fast to maintain a longer stride, shorten your stride or select a more appropriate song.

- *Body focus 4.* Count out your cadence aloud with each stride.

- *Body focus 5.* Pay attention to the rotation of your torso as your arm swings and the tip makes contact. Allow your lower body to follow the path of the pole, and then counter with effort in the upper body.

Cool-Down: Take five minutes to cool down and stretch.

PART III

Programming for Long-Term Goals

CHAPTER 14

Training for Cardio Health and Fitness

In the past 20 years, government agencies and the medical community have made great strides in affirming the positive effects of cardiorespiratory exercise on health, such as reducing the risk of coronary artery disease and increasing capacity for exercise, endurance, and the strength of skeletal muscles. Because Nordic walking simultaneously uses most of the body's large muscles, it fits the bill perfectly. The following programs outline how to most efficiently move those muscle groups while Nordic walking.

Table 14.1 outlines some of the beneficial physiological changes that occur in the body as a result of regular aerobic exercise. Note that once you have made these changes over a period of weeks and months, you can maintain your new level of fitness by exercising just two days per week. However, competitive athletes should train at least two to four days per week to maintain their edge and fine-tune technique. Competition events count as training days. To maintain peak performance, athletes should perform workouts of a higher intensity for a shorter period of time and should take days off for recovery. It is much easier to maintain a certain level of fitness than it is to work toward significant improvements. However, if you stop exercising completely, your fitness level will drop quickly. Your gains will begin to diminish within 48 hours and will be lost within 5 to 10 weeks. Observe the following exercise programs to maintain these physiological adaptations.

Table 14.1   Results of Regular Cardiorespiratory Training

Adaptation	Result
Strength of heart muscles ↑	Heart beats fewer times to circulate the same amount of blood. Heart able to circulate more blood at a higher rate.
Capillary density and size ↑	Greater exchange of oxygen between blood and cells. Body can use more of the oxygen being circulated.
Hemoglobin amounts ↑	Body can carry more oxygen from the blood to the working muscles.
Capacity for oxygen consumption ↑ ($\dot{V}O_2$)	You can exercise longer and at a higher level before growing fatigued.
Lactate threshold ↑	You can exercise longer and at a higher level before growing fatigued.

Assessing Fitness

You are obviously making progress if you can tolerate greater distances or speeds without experiencing muscular discomfort or severe breathlessness. Assess your physical feedback after every workout to see whether you should scale back the intensity. If you routinely experience discomfort in one of the training categories, go back to the previous level and establish a good base of fitness before progressing. You must listen to your body, since pushing too hard leads to overuse injuries and a variety of overtraining symptoms. Chapter 17 discusses symptoms of overtraining, as well as strategies to minimize its occurrence.

Another physiological marker of fitness level is your resting heart rate. Resting heart rates range from 50 to 90 beats per minute. Walkers with greater cardiorespiratory health typically land in the lower end of the spectrum. Highly trained endurance athletes may even have resting heart rates between 30 to 50 beats per minute. Measure your heart rate in the morning before you get out of bed for an accurate reading. Average the readings after five to seven days. Once you have established a baseline, you can take your heart rate daily or weekly to gauge your body's response to subsequent training. For example, a lower resting heart rate may signify improved fitness and an increase in the efficiency of your cardiorespiratory system as your heart increases in size and pumps more blood with each beat. On the other hand, overtraining, dehydration, inadequate rest and recovery, emotional stress, poor nutritional status, altitude, or medications can lead to higher resting heart rates. In general, you should monitor any changes from the baseline measure and make adjustments accordingly. Even a resting heart rate of 5 beats higher than normal can indicate

Courtesy of www.markjobeimages.com.

Once you're proficient, it's challenging to synchronize your strides with other walkers to improve balance, agility, and coordination. But it can also be fun and can take your mind off of the intensity of training.

that you may not be ready for a high-intensity or challenging workout, so it may be best to choose a low-intensity routine. When competitive athletes feel great, they may want to push hard during every workout, but this practice can diminish performance and even be dangerous. Resting heart rate provides a window into the needs of your body and can be an essential guide for making immediate and future program modifications.

In addition to resting heart rate, recovery heart rate is a very good indicator of cardiovascular fitness. Recovery heart rate refers to the number of beats the heart drops during 1 minute immediately after an exercise bout. In general, the heart rate of a very fit person will drop more quickly than that of a less fit individual. The quick drop in heart rate in a fit person enables the ability to quickly do work again in a short period of time and in repeated bouts. Some research even suggests that a slower heart rate recovery after exercise may be a strong predictor of mortality. So not only is it important to improve your body's recovery response for performance, but also potentially for health as well. Using a heart rate monitor during interval training (as seen in chapter 2) is the best method to train and track this physiologic response. As a general guideline, a drop in heart rate of 30 beats after 1 minute of reduced intensity is an indicator of poor fitness. On the other hand, a drop of 50 beats after 1 minute indicates excellent fitness. Another method of assessing recovery is to mark the total elapsed time it takes for your heart rate to drop to your resting heart rate. Dropping to your resting heart rate within 60 seconds is considered good, where a 30 second elapsed time is considered excellent. Be sure to track recovery heart rate during intense interval-type training, or simply at the end of any workout to get another picture of your overall level of fitness.

Another method for measuring progress is to periodically perform fitness assessments. Use the assessments in chapter 7 every four to six weeks to gauge your improvement. The results will either validate your workout routine or motivate you to keep working toward your goals. If your results indicate that you have graduated to a new category, begin following the appropriate routine.

The following training programs reflect exercise routines for the Nordic walking categories outlined in chapter 7, including skill development, fitness proficiency, and competition. Each category has two four-week programs with workouts from part II that are progressively challenging. Therefore, even though you may have initially tested for one category, with time and improvement, you can move into the next category. The average volume is three to five routines of 20 to 120 minutes and the average intensity is 55 to 90 percent of maximum heart rate. The weekly workouts intentionally vary the intensity to maximize your motivation and enjoyment. Additionally, all programs include multiple recovery days. If you are interested in cross-training or supplemental activities, you may introduce them on off days as long as you take one or two days of true rest each week. While the primary objective of this chapter is pure cardio submersion, it also offers fun outdoor options to add a little variety in the bootcamp, freestyle, and flow workouts. Chapters 16 and 17 discuss cross-training and supplemental activities. Remember that the total workout time listed does not include warm-up and cool-down periods.

Skill Development Programs

Use this category if both assessments in chapter 7 rated you as a beginning Nordic walker. Focus on enhancing your technique before improving your speed or endurance. Nordic walking consistently several times a week will certainly help you develop confidence and efficiency with the poles. If your practice is consistent, the momentum will motivate you to do more. Use the following programs, of moderate volume and intensity, to establish a solid base of cardiorespiratory fitness, minimize injury, and prepare your body for more intense programs in the future.

SKILL DEVELOPMENT PROGRAM I

These workouts allow you to simultaneously learn Nordic walking skills and ease into the new cardiorespiratory demands of the activity. Take time to develop the relationship between the pole tip and the walking surface, which creates forward momentum. Remember that tip contact inspires stride length. Progressing stride length over a period of eight weeks, instead of overnight, is the secret to preventing injury. These workouts are wonderful for athletes who are pregnant or are undergoing physical therapy.

General Program Design

Frequency: Three or four days per week

Intensity: 55 to 70 percent HRmax

Pace: Low to moderate

Type: Nordic walking mainly on flat and even surfaces

Time: 20 to 50 minutes

	Sun	Mon	Tue	Wed	Thu	Fri	Sat
Week 1	Off	Short and easy 1	Off	Short and easy 2	Off	Short and easy 3	Off
Week 2	Off	Short and easy 2	Off	Short and easy 3	Off	Short and easy 4	Off
Week 3	Off	Short and easy 3	Off	Off	Short and easy 4	Off	Medium and steady 1
Week 4	Off	Off	Short and easy 2	Off	Medium and steady 1	Off	Medium and steady 2

Note: Refer to part II for individual workout details.

SKILL DEVELOPMENT PROGRAM II

These workouts focus on skill development and increase intensity and difficulty to prepare you for fitness proficiency programs.

General Program Design

Frequency: Three or four days per week

Intensity: 55 to 75 percent HRmax

Pace: Low to moderate

Type: Nordic walking mainly on flat and even surfaces

Time: 30 to 75 minutes

	Sun	Mon	Tue	Wed	Thu	Fri	Sat
Week 1	Off	Off	Short and easy 5	Off	Short and easy 6	Off	Medium and steady 2
Week 2	Off	Short and easy 7	Off	Short and easy 5	Off	Off	Long and steady 1
Week 3	Off	Short and easy 8	Medium and steady 3	Off	Medium and steady 5	Off	Medium and steady 1
Week 4	Off	Medium and steady 6	Short and easy 7	Off	Medium and steady 4	Off	Long and steady 2

Note: Refer to part II for individual workout details.

Fitness Proficiency Programs

Work in this category if both assessments in chapter 7 rated you as average. At this level, you should have a general base of cardiorespiratory conditioning, which provides a springboard for the workout schedule. If you have never Nordic walked before, you will learn skills that enhance your technique quickly. To advance, you must ensure that your form is sound and efficient before attempting significant increases in speed and distance. Since you are using all major muscle groups, you will burn lots of calories and will achieve great cardiorespiratory conditioning.

The following programs are of moderate-to-high volume and intensity. This is a clear departure from the skill development workouts, which focus on increasing strength and speed. In order to stay on schedule with this demanding routine, you must plan to take days off.

FITNESS PROFICIENCY PROGRAM I

These textbook cardio workouts are geared to maintain your heart rate by gradually increasing the intensity. The moderate and constant pace should keep your RPE between 4 and 6. Your objective is to accomplish steady-state training for a prolonged period of time. You will walk on varied terrain, including dirt roads and inclines. Learn to be more creative with your outdoor path with freestyle 1, and get in touch with each footstep with an option for flow 1.

General Program Design

Frequency: Four or five days per week

Intensity: 65 to 80 percent HRmax

Pace: Moderate to fast

Type: Nordic walking on flat surfaces with some inclines

Time: 30 to 150 minutes

	Sun	Mon	Tue	Wed	Thu	Fri	Sat
Week 1	Off	Medium and steady 2	Off	Medium and steady 1	Medium and steady 7	Off	Long and steady 3
Week 2	Off	Off	Medium and quick 1	Off	Medium and quick 2	Medium and quick 3	Long and steady 2
Week 3	Off	Medium and quick 4	Short and easy 5	Freestyle 1	Off	Medium and steady 8	Long and steady 6
Week 4	Off	Short and easy 7	Medium and quick 7	Off	Medium and steady 8	Short and easy 5 or Flow 1	Medium and quick 5

Note: Refer to part II for individual workout details.

FITNESS PROFICIENCY PROGRAM II

These workouts are a little more intense in terms of heart rate, RPE, and pace. Focus on developing your pace for athletic training as you learn speed technique. You will work out on a variety of surfaces and be ready for a slightly more interval workout during boot camp 1 and 2. Perform three strength-training workouts each week.

General Program Design

Frequency: Four or five days per week

Intensity: 65 to 80 percent HRmax

Pace: Moderate to fast

Type: Nordic walking on flat surfaces with some inclines

Time: 30 to 180 minutes

	Sun	Mon	Tue	Wed	Thu	Fri	Sat
Week 1	Off	Medium and steady 5	Off	Short and fast 2	Medium and quick 8	Off	Long and steady 7
Week 2	Off	Boot camp 1	Off	Medium and quick 5	Short and fast 6	Off	Long and steady 6
Week 3	Off	Medium and quick 7	Short and fast 1	Short and easy 7	Medium and steady 7	Off	Short and fast 6
Week 4	Off	Boot camp 2	Short and easy 8	Short and fast 8	Off	Short and easy 4 or Flow 1	Medium and quick 4

Note: Refer to part II for individual workout details.

Competition Programs

Work on this category if both assessments from chapter 7 rated you as advanced. At this level, your highly efficient technique should allow you to achieve speed and distance with fluidity. You should be able to fully engage the major muscle groups of both the upper and lower body to maximize propulsion and caloric expenditure.

After the athlete has sufficiently built a base of solid endurance and strength, the purpose of the competition period is for the athlete to focus on peaking for an event. This is accomplished by a low volume of training combined with very high-intensity training that is focused on sport-specific technique. Not only does this help keep skills refined and sharp for an upcoming competition, but it also prevents overtraining. The long and steady workouts are intended as placeholders for competitive events. See chapters 12 and 13 for additional programming ideas that will enhance your performance.

COMPETITION PROGRAM I

Assume an athletic mindset and change up your pace by using speed technique with any cardio workout. Look for steeper hills when a workout calls for an incline. Relish in the outdoor experience as you run slalom through trees. At the same time, competition phases get less intense so you can save your strength for the real deal—competition.

General Program Design

Frequency: Three or four days per week

Intensity: 60 to 90 percent HRmax

Pace: Moderate to fast

Type: Nordic walking on flat, uneven, and hilly terrain. You may choose to cross-train during the week with swimming, in-line skating, or cycling, but you should substitute those activities for steady or easy workouts to adhere to the schedule. Flow 2 and freestyle 1 add elements of strength and body awareness to your workouts.

Time: 25 to 180 minutes

	Sun	Mon	Tue	Wed	Thu	Fri	Sat
Week 1	Off	Medium and quick 8	Off	Short and fast 5	Off or Flow 1	Off	Long and steady 6 or competitive event
Week 2	Off or Flow 2	Off	Medium and steady 7	Off	Off	Short and easy 7 or Flow 1	Medium and quick 3
Week 3	Off	Short and fast 6	Freestyle 1	Short and easy 8	Off	Off	Long and steady 7 or competitive event
Week 4	Off	Boot camp 1	Medium and quick 5	Short and easy 3 or Flow 1	Off	Off	Medium and steady 8

Note: Refer to part II for individual workout details

COMPETITION PROGRAM II

These workouts, which are inspired by adventure racing, emphasize both intensity and cardiorespiratory endurance. The rugged terrain is modified for Nordic walking. Take three or four rest days each week to compensate for the intensity of the regimen.

General Program Design

Frequency: Three or four days per week

Intensity: 60 to 90 percent HRmax

Pace: Moderate to fast

Type: Nordic walking on flat, uneven, and hilly terrain. You may choose to cross-train several days a week with swimming, in-line skating, or cycling, but you should substitute those activities for steady or easy workouts to adhere to the schedule.

Time: 30 to 200 minutes

	Sun	Mon	Tue	Wed	Thu	Fri	Sat
Week 1	Off	Boot camp 2	Off	Short and easy 4	Off	Short and fast 4	Long and steady 8 or competitive event
Week 2	Off	Off or Flow 1	Medium and quick 3	Off	Short and easy 6	Off	Medium and steady 8 or Flow 3
Week 3	Off	Medium and steady 6	Off	Short and easy 5 or Flow 1	Off	Medium and quick 7	Short and fast 6
Week 4	Off or Flow 2	Short and easy 2	Off	Short and easy 6	Freestyle 2	Off	Long and steady 3 or competitive event

Note: Refer to part II for individual workout details.

CHAPTER 15

Targeting Total-Body Fitness

A complete training program for Nordic walking results in total-body fitness. Whether you're using Nordic walking to cross-train for another sport or as the staple of your fitness activity, this chapter trains the full body for static and dynamic balance, agility, coordination, and power. The six four-week programs feature creative workouts from part II, including circuit, boot-camp, freestyle, and flow workouts. Of the six programs, two are designated for each of the fitness categories (skill development, fitness proficiency, and competition). All the programs include rest days. This book designates Sunday as the generic day of rest, but you can change it to suit your particular needs.

The following programs follow ACSM guidelines and include drills for cardiorespiratory endurance, strength, agility, and flexibility. The intensity of these programs is progressive, so Fitness Proficiency II is more challenging than Fitness Proficiency I. If you are a fitness enthusiast but a beginning Nordic walker, you may prefer to start with the section on skill development and work your way up. When you can comfortably accomplish both of the programs in a given level, move on to the next level.

Select strength exercises that complement your stride to prevent overuse injuries. Also remember to focus on muscles that are somewhat neglected during walking, such as the abductors and adductors. Although they actively stabilize your thighs during walking, these support muscles often go unnoticed until you start to feel sore after a long walk. You should also strengthen the

A complete training program for Nordic walking results in total-body fitness.

hamstrings, forearms, lower legs, and upper back. Because Nordic walking uses all major muscle groups, incorporating these muscles protects your knees and directly enhance stride mechanics.

Refer to the following guidelines when performing the programs in this chapter:

- *Strength training.* During skill development workouts, do one set of 8 to 10 strength-training exercises, with 8 to 12 repetitions of each exercise. Perform this workout, which should last approximately 20 minutes, twice a week.

- *Easy activity.* Perform these low-intensity activities for 30 minutes. Examples include walking the dog, stretching, doing Pilates, or any activity that moves your body through a comfortable range of motion.

- *Moderate recreational activity.* Work out for 45 minutes with activities such as swimming, playing paddle ball at the beach, golfing, in-line skating on flat terrain, or cycling. Any activity aimed at fun and participation that requires movement and energy can be appropriate.

Skill Development Programs

These programs will ease you into Nordic walking and will help you improve skills, strengthen your heart, move safely between levels, and establish an efficient walking groove for working smarter and harder. You should walk two to three times each week. The average walking workout is 40 minutes long, not including warm-up and cool-down times. These workouts are supplemented with two strength-training routines per week. These easier workouts from chapters 8, 9, and 13 are appropriate for anyone who is pregnant or recovering from injury. You may perform them on your lunch hour or during a rest day if you are already pretty fit.

SKILL DEVELOPMENT PROGRAM I

These workouts allow you to simultaneously learn Nordic walking skills and ease into the new cardiorespiratory demands of the activity. Take time to develop the relationship between the pole tip and the walking surface, which creates forward momentum. Remember that tip contact inspires stride length. Progressing stride length over a period of eight weeks, instead of overnight, is the secret to preventing injury. These workouts are wonderful for athletes who are pregnant or are undergoing physical therapy. You'll experience flow 1, a relaxing walk for rest days.

General Program Design

Frequency: Mix two or three sessions of Nordic walking with strength training and easy or moderate activity. Take at least one day off per week.

Intensity: 55 to 65 percent HRmax

Pace: Easy

RPE: 2 to 4

Time (average): 35 minutes per workout

	Sun	Mon	Tue	Wed	Thu	Fri	Sat	Total time	RPE
Week 1	Off	Short and easy 2	Off	Strength training	Flow 1	Strength training	Easy activity	160	2-3
Week 2	Off	Easy activity	Short and easy 4	Strength training	Off	Strength training	Short and easy 5	135	2-4
Week 3	Off	Short and easy 3	Easy activity	Strength training	Flow 1	Strength training	Medium and steady 2	175	3-4
Week 4	Off	Easy activity	Medium and steady 2	Strength training	Off	Strength training	Medium and steady 1	180	3-4

Note: Refer to part II for details of individual workouts.

SKILL DEVELOPMENT PROGRAM II

These workouts focus on skill development and increase intensity and difficulty to prepare you for the fitness proficiency programs. You'll also experience flow 2, a meditative walking workout.

General Program Design

Frequency: Mix two or three sessions of Nordic walking with strength training and easy or moderate activity. Take at least one day off per week.

Intensity: 55 to 70 percent HRmax

Pace: Easy to moderate

RPE: 3 to 6

Time (average): 45 minutes per workout

	Sun	Mon	Tue	Wed	Thu	Fri	Sat	Total time	RPE
Week 1	Off	Strength training	Medium and steady 2	Strength training	Off	Moderate activity	Flow 1	195	3-4
Week 2	Off	Medium and quick 1	Moderate activity	Strength training	Off	Strength training	Short and easy 6	175	3-5
Week 3	Off	Strength training	Short and easy 7	Strength training	Easy activity	Medium and quick 2	Moderate activity	210	3-6
Week 4	Off	Medium and quick 3	Strength training	Flow 2	Strength training	Off	Medium and steady 5	220	4-6

Note: Refer to part II for details of individual workouts.

Fitness Proficiency Programs

Use these programs if you enjoy regular workouts and have specific goals like weight loss or cardiorespiratory maintenance. The three or four walking workouts per week last for about an average of 60 minutes and keep your heart rate at a moderate intensity. If you hope to lose weight, you must supplement walking routines with activities that raise your heart rate and eat appropriate portions of complex carbohydrates and lean proteins.

Days of strength training and easy-to-moderate activity round out the routine. For active rest days, consider flow 1, 2, or 3. During fitness proficiency workouts, perform two sets of 8 to 10 strength-training exercises, with 10 to 12 repetitions of each drill. Do these sets twice a week for approximately 30 minutes.

FITNESS PROFICIENCY PROGRAM I

These textbook cardio workouts are geared to maintain your heart rate by gradually increasing the intensity. The moderate and constant pace should keep your RPE between 3 and 7. Your objective is to accomplish steady-state training for a prolonged period of time. You will walk on varied terrain, including dirt roads and inclines.

General Program Design

Frequency: Mix three sessions of Nordic walking with strength training and easy or moderate activity. Take at least one day off per week. On active recovery days, do flow 1 or another easy activity.

Intensity: 55 to 80 percent HRmax

Pace: Easy to mostly moderate

Time (average): 60 minutes per workout

	Sun	Mon	Tue	Wed	Thu	Fri	Sat	Total time	RPE
Week 1	Off	Flow 2	Strength training	Medium and steady 2	Strength training	Easy activity	Medium and quick 3	260	3-6
Week 2	Off	Strength training	Long and steady 2	Flow 1	Strength training	Medium and steady 7	Moderate activity	282	4-6
Week 3	Off	Strength training	Medium and quick 5	Strength training	Free-style 1	Easy activity	Medium and steady 8	270	4-6
Week 4	Off	Short and fast 2	Strength training	Long and steady 4	Easy activity	Flow 2	Strength training	275	4-7

Note: Refer to part II for details of individual workouts.

FITNESS PROFICIENCY II

These workouts are a little more intense in terms of heart rate, RPE, and pace. Focus on developing your pace for athletic training as you learn speed technique. You will work out on a variety of surfaces during boot camp 1. Perform two strength-training workouts each week. As the weeks progress, you will gradually incorporate boot-camp and freestyle workouts.

General Program Design

Frequency: Mix three or four sessions of Nordic walking with strength training and moderate activity. Take at least one day off per week. On active recovery days, do flow 1 or another easy activity.

Intensity: 60 to 75 percent HRmax

Pace: Moderate to fast

Time (average): 65 minutes per workout

	Sun	Mon	Tue	Wed	Thu	Fri	Sat	Total time	RPE
Week 1	Off	Medium and steady 3	Strength training	Medium and quick 5	Strength training	Long and steady 2	Flow 2	317	4-7
Week 2	Off	Strength training	Flow 2	Strength training	Medium and steady 7	Moderate activity	Long and steady 3	330	4-7
Week 3	Off	Medium and quick 6	Strength training	Boot camp 1	Flow 2	Strength training	Medium and steady 7	330	5-7
Week 4	Off	Strength training	Short and fast 1	Moderate activity	Free-style 2	Strength training	Long and steady 6	362	5-7

Note: Refer to part II for details of individual workouts.

Competition Programs

Use these programs if you wish to take your training to a new level of intensity and enhance agility, coordination, and power. Incorporate high-impact workouts to push your athletic potential. Flow workouts 1, 2, and 3 are interspersed on days of active rest.

COMPETITION PROGRAM I

Assume an athletic mindset and change up your pace by using speed technique with any cardio workout. Look for steeper hills when a workout calls for an incline. Relish in the outdoor experience as you perform push-ups on benches and step-ups on curbs or run slalom through trees. This playful level utilizes the best of chapter 13. Think of your neighborhood, local park, or walking path as an adventure zone for training. As in previous competition workouts, program 1 utilizes specific days for strength-training drills that relate to your goals. A general program includes two or three sets of 8 to 10 exercises. Perform these routines, which should last for 45 minutes, twice weekly.

General Program Design

Frequency: Mix four sessions of Nordic walking with strength-training workouts, such as boot camp and freestyle, each week. Take at least one day of active rest to perform flow 1, an easy activity, or any workout from chapter 8.

Intensity: 60 to 80 percent HRmax

Pace: Moderate to fast

Time (average): 70 minutes per workout

	Sun	Mon	Tue	Wed	Thu	Fri	Sat	Total time	RPE
Week 1	Off	Strength training	Medium and steady 6	Flow 2	Strength training	Boot camp 1	Long and steady 5	375	4-7
Week 2	Off	Strength training	Short and fast 5	Strength training	Freestyle 1	Short and easy 5	Long and steady 6	367	5-8
Week 3	Off	Boot camp 2	Medium and quick 3	Long and steady 3	Flow 1	Strength training	Medium and steady 8	380	6-9
Week 4	Off	Short and fast 7	Freestyle 2	Moderate activity	Medium and quick 8	Flow 2	Boot camp 1	360	6-8

Note: Refer to part II for details of individual workouts.

COMPETITION PROGRAM II

These workouts, which are inspired by adventure racing, emphasize both intensity and cardiorespiratory endurance, less the gnarly terrain! Strength training takes place during freestyle and boot-camp workouts. Take two rest days each week to compensate for the intensity of the regimen.

General Program Design

Frequency: Mix four or five sessions of Nordic walking with strength-training workouts, such as boot camp and freestyle. Take at least one day of active rest to perform flow 1, an easy activity, or any workout from chapter 8.

Intensity: 65 to 90 percent HRmax

Pace: Moderate to fast

Time (average): 75 minutes per workout.

	Sun	Mon	Tue	Wed	Thu	Fri	Sat	Total time	RPE
Week 1	Off	Long and steady 7	Short and easy 6	Freestyle 2	Off	Short and fast 7	Medium and steady 8	390	5-7
Week 2	Off	Freestyle 2	Medium and quick 7	Boot camp 1	Short and fast 8	Moderate activity	Flow 3	370	5-8
Week 3	Off	Freestyle 2	Short and fast 6	Long and steady 6	Off	Boot camp 2	Medium and quick 5	417	6-9
Week 4	Off	Boot camp 2	Medium and quick 7	Long and steady 8	Off	Freestyle 1	Flow 3	530	5-9

Note: Refer to part II for details of individual workouts.

CHAPTER 16

Cross-Training for Sports

You may be surprised to learn that road biking and in-line skating have much in common with Nordic walking. Nordic walking is an excellent way to cross-train for other sports. In turn, the road biker who cross-trains with Nordic walking gains forward momentum, activating the core, which makes the upper and middle torso more functional for riding. These activities are a good match for cross-training because of the repetitive opposition of the upper and lower body. Other obvious matches for Nordic walking include cross-country skiing and running.

Cross-training increases your fitness levels beyond what you would be achieve with Nordic walking alone, making your body more versatile, responsive, and efficient. You will reduce your potential for injury, especially the over- and repetitive-use injuries that are commonly experienced in endurance activities.

Training Principles

You can expect to improve your cardiorespiratory proficiency, core strength, and fitness capacity by doing other sports. Cross-training produces physiological adaptations that are necessary for speed, technique, and efficient oxygen utilization. Adapting to the stresses of training minimizes the risk of fatigue and injury. Consider the principles of the following sections to adapt practically and safely.

Adaptation

When you repeat the demand of a movement over and over, your body learns to recognize it and to associate it with specific activity. Cross-training produces progressive and natural adaptations of the circulatory, muscular, and nervous systems. Muscle memory is also enhanced. As you become stronger and more skilled, your nerves carry impulses more freely to the working muscles, which makes familiar movements more coordinated. For example, world-class distance runners at the top of their games may initially be uncoordinated as cross-country skiers. Adaptation is specific to the individual; you will progress in your own time. The end result of adaptation is that your body performs the movement or task efficiently.

Overload

For improvement to take place, workloads must continually impose demands on your muscles and energy systems. As your body adapts to increased loads, add even more load. Increasing the intensity, frequency, or duration of your activities will improve fitness. Monitor your heart rate to measure gains from overload and adaptation to exercise. For example, as fitness levels improve, resting heart rate decreases. Therefore, to maintain a specific heart rate, you have to work harder. When the task no longer taxes your energy system, add more load.

Specificity

The training principle of specificity dictates that your training should reflect the biomechanical nature and physiological demands of Nordic walking. Difficulties arise when opposing demands are placed on your cross-training activities. For example, leg strength and endurance developed through cycling transfers easily to Alpine skiing. However, the stop-and-go nature of Alpine skiing can have a negative effect on the road-biking skills of endurance and speed. The downside of cross-training is that your body may lose skills that are specific to your sport. In order to maintain efficiency, continue practicing your primary sport or cross-train with one that closely duplicates it. Cross-country skiing is a perfect match for Nordic walking.

The four-week programs in this chapter should inspire cross-country skiers, cyclists, and runners to pick up Nordic walking poles. Each program includes at least one weekly rest day. Sunday is the generic rest day for these programs, but feel free to change the schedule to meet your particular needs. The time assessments do not include warm-up and cool-down periods.

Assess Your Sport

How similar is your favorite sport to Nordic walking? Here are a few guidelines for assessing sports for specific qualities that complement Nordic walking. For example, even though rock climbing is completely different from Nordic walking, the cardiorespiratory nature and range of motion of both activities are highly compatible. Cyclists appreciate the opportunity to train in a different movement pattern and skiers appreciate getting out of the snow while getting a specific workout.

Most sports fit into one of three categories:

1. Human-powered sports with continuous forward motion, such as swimming, running, skating, road cycling, and cross-country skiing. All of these activities develop both aerobic and anaerobic capacity that is comparable to Nordic training goals that are more intense. These sports are classically aerobic, and can be pushed even further with interval training. Nordic walking is an excellent cross-training activity for these sports.

2. Sports that require slightly longer bursts of energy with only brief pauses between them develop higher levels of aerobic fitness. Examples include soccer, tennis, and handball. These sports combine aerobic and anaerobic conditioning. An athlete can reach any level of intensity while Nordic walking. Anaerobic training and intervals enhance cardio proficiency on the field. Nordic walkers who wish to be competitive in these sports will fare well by adding these activities to their training programs.

3. Sports that require extremely short bursts of exertion with long pauses between rely almost exclusively on anaerobic mechanisms, which produce energy without the presence of oxygen. Examples include softball, football, and volleyball. These sports confer little aerobic benefit, and are sure to take your breath away because they are anaerobic in nature. Although it is possible to train at this intensity, Nordic walking does not match the sport skills, muscle recruitment, and playing intensity of these sports. In this light, Nordic walking could be exactly what the coach ordered for these athletes in terms of active rest. Many high-intensity sports require sudden stopping, starting, pivoting, and dodging, which prevents automation of movement. Athletes in these sports should pick up Nordic poles at least once a week to work on symmetry, rhythm, and cadence, the trademarks of natural movement and walking.

Chart your sport

The following sports chart (table 16.1, page 190) can help you decide which sports are most compatible with Nordic walking. Sport skills are accomplished with awareness of these five performance variables. The best way to make this assessment is to watch live practices or videos of your sports.

All sports include varying degrees of these five performance variables:

• *Balance.* Equilibrium is facilitated in part by your stance and posture. Where is the center of mass in relation to the feet during movement? Are weight transfers (from foot to foot) constant or erratic, moving in a variety of directions? Imagine a soccer player who moves all over the field, making rapid changes in direction. Ice hockey is a better match in terms of cross-training. Equestrian sports are well suited for cross-training with Nordic walking. Like Nordic walking, equestrian sports keep the center of mass neutral while moving forward.

- *Space.* To determine the amount of space you need, evaluate the direction of your movements and the range of motion needed to accomplish sport skills and actions. Sports that emphasize movement from the hips and shoulders, such as running, are compatible with Nordic walking.

- *Strength.* How much effort is required to accomplish individual sport skills? This effort relates to both energy demands and accurate range of motion. Is a golfer's swing similar to Nordic walking? Although both activities require long arms, flexed elbows, and neutral wrists, the ranges of motion are not complementary. Tennis would be a better match for golf, but neither sport is a good match for Nordic walking.

- *Speed.* How fast is the body moving as a whole? What is the quality of the speed when you break the movements down? What is the velocity and timing of each movement? Consider an in-line skater who moves forward with momentum and velocity, the prerequisites for speed. The energy demands and forward propulsion of this sport make it a close match with Nordic walking that should produce wonderful cardiorespiratory results. Leg and arm movements are extended and long in both sports.

- *Energy demands.* Different sports place different cardiorespiratory demands on the body. Is yours a stop-and-go sport or is it nonstop? Is it aerobic or anaerobic? Are there short bursts of intense effort or is effort comfortable? This chapter discusses this element of training at great length.

In the table sport-specific ratings are on a scale of 1 to 5 where 1 is not specific at all and 5 is very specific. A rating of *complimentary* means that although not as specific, conditioning with activities and exercises that may be similar to your sport of choice is always positive. The beauty of cross-training is that you can work muscle groups that Nordic walking doesn't activate. For example, although golfing does not look like Nordic walking, practicing the swing enhances shoulder strength and range of motion. A rating of *good* means it is a step up from complimentary, these activities are a better match to meet your goals. *Very good* activities are a close match in terms of energy consumption and muscle use. *Excellent* activities are the most specific, and make excellent crossover sports for Nordic walking.

In this table, cross-country skiing only received a rating of 4+ because its speed is greater than that of fitness walking with poles. However, because poles are used in a similar capacity (responding to resistance from tips and the surface) for both sports, enabling very specific torso movements, terrific cardiorespiratory conditioning, and forward propulsion, this sport is as specific as it gets!

Fitness walking the old-fashioned way, without poles, is the single most popular cardiorespiratory exercise. Why did it receive a rating of 4? Without the use of poles, there is little resistance in the upper body. In a sense, fitness walking is only half the workout that Nordic walking is. Still, Nordic walking could not exist without it, so it deserves an honorable mention!

Table 16.1 Sport-specific Cross-training

Activity	Balance	Space	Strength	Speed	Energy	Sport specific rating
Cycling	Very good	Good	Very good	Complimentary	Excellent	4
Cross-country skiing	Excellent	Very good	Excellent	Very good	Excellent	4+
Alpine skiing	Complimentary	Complimentary	Very good	Complimentary	Good	3
In-line skating (forward stride)	Very good	Very good	Very good	Good	Excellent	4
Running	Very good	Very good	Very good	Very good	Excellent	4
Golf	Complimentary	Complimentary	Very good	Complimentary	Complimentary	2+
Soccer	Complimentary	Good	Very good	Good	Very good	3-
Yoga	Very good	Complimentary	Excellent	Complimentary	Good	3
Equestrian	Very good	Complimentary	Complimentary	Complimentary	Good	2+
Bowling	Good	Very good	Complimentary	Complimentary	Complimentary	2
Swimming	Good	Very good	Very good	Good	Excellent	3+
Walking (no poles)	Excellent	Very good	Very good	Very good	Very good	4
Backpacking	Complimentary	Good	Very good	Good	Very good	3
Trekking (with poles)	Very good	Good	Excellent	Good	Very good	3+
Hiking	Good	Good	Very good	Good	Very good	3
Snowshoeing (no poles)	Good	Good	Good	Complimentary	Very good	3-

Just because trekking and Nordic walking both use poles does not mean that the workouts are the same. First, the equipment is designed differently. Second, the terrain where trekking poles are used is the opposite of Nordic walking. Trekking is a stop-and-go activity that uses poles for survival! Narrow trails make it difficult to reach a training heart rate. Heart rate usually increases because of altitude gain or steepness of terrain.

Programs

The following cross-training programs follow ACSM guidelines. They include training for cardiorespiratory endurance, strength, and flexibility, as well as agility and plyometric drills. They are recommended for cross-country skiers, cyclists, and runners as an addition to or an alternative to their typical training regimes. Each has a different theme. All three programs are presented in four-week cycles, and possess similar qualities of fitness:

1. The cardiorespiratory system is the primary beneficiary of your effort.
2. Drills to enhance upper-body strength are prevalent to produce muscle balance and prevent injuries.
3. Efficient and rhythmic forward movements are used to increase intensity.
4. Energetic routines, including boot-camp, freestyle, and flow workouts provide full-body training.

CROSS-COUNTRY SKIING PROGRAM: A PERFECT COMPLIMENT

Nordic walking is the closest specific match to cross-country skiing in terms of movement and equipment. After all, Nordic walking was invented by cross-country skiers. The main difference is terrain! Snow and high altitudes also add resistance, making cross-country skiing the more intense of the two sports. If you are a skier, Nordic walking can complement your skills and enhance your energy systems.

Another major difference between the two sports is glide time, which doesn't take place in Nordic walking. There are no short delays in movement like during a skier's glide phase. At the end of each stride, cross-country skiers glide forward on the snow, giving muscles of the upper and lower body a momentary break. These few seconds also give skiers time to follow through on the back swing, releasing the poles completely. Skiers who try Nordic walking should work on lengthening their stride to make time for the release. This process takes time, and may produce injuries to the groin and lower back if you are not careful. Concentrate on passively releasing the pole by simply relaxing your hand as it passes by your hip.

General Program Design

Objective: Ease the transition from land to snow with this preseason dry-land routine. As the RPE and distance increase, focus on building strength and cardiorespiratory endurance.

Frequency: Five or six times per week

Intensity: Moderate to fast

Time (average): 60 to 75 minutes per workout

	Sun	Mon	Tue	Wed	Thu	Fri	Sat	Total time	RPE
Week 1	Off	Medium and steady 5	Strength training: 30 min	Flow 2	Boot camp 1	Long and steady 1	Strength training: 30 min	360	5-7
Week 2	Off	Strength training: 30 min	Medium and quick 5	Freestyle 1	Long and steady 5	Medium and steady 4	Strength training: 30 min	330	5-7
Week 3	Off	Long and steady 3	Medium and steady 1	Strength training: 30 min	Medium and steady 7	Short and fast 3	Freestyle 2	315	6-7
Week 4	Off	Medium and steady 7	Long and steady 4	Boot camp 1	Flow 1	Medium and quick 6	Strength training: 30 min	370	7-8

CYCLING PROGRAM: INSURANCE FOR PERFORMANCE

Cyclists can cross-train with Nordic walking midseason to increase upper-body strength and to develop a movement pattern that complements the muscle use and function of cycling. Cycling and Nordic walking share the trademarks of forward propulsion and cardiorespiratory endurance. Both sports rely on lightweight equipment. The difference is that the upper body drives the Nordic walking stride, and the lower body drives the bike forward. Therefore, Nordic walking can provide some much-needed balance to the muscular system.

Nordic walking reestablishes core and torso rotation, which cyclists often lose while riding. Activating core muscles can help you literally relax during long rides. As you spread the effort throughout your body, you will enhance endurance and reduce your perceived exertion, enlivening muscles that might have otherwise been dormant. Increased core strength reduces pain and numbness in the lower back, and helps prevent overuse injuries caused by repetitive motion and muscle weakness.

Since cycling includes periods of rest, the following workouts reflect varying heart rates but stay in a zone that is compatible with the bulk of your training.

The primary benefits of this program are back strength and muscle balance.

General Program Design

Objective: This routine is for the middle of the cycling season. Focus on training the muscles of the torso, core, and back for maximum balance.

Frequency: Five or six times per week

Intensity: Moderate to fast

Time (average): 50 to 77 minutes per workout

	Sun	Mon	Tue	Wed	Thu	Fri	Sat	Total time	RPE
Week 1	Off	Timed cycling: 60 min	Freestyle 1	Timed cycling: 60 min	Strength training: 30 min	Medium and quick 4	Timed cycling: 75 min	345	5-6
Week 2	Off	Strength training: 30 min	Timed cycling: 90 min	Boot camp 1	Timed cycling: 75 min	Medium and steady 7	Timed cycling: 60 min	375	5-7
Week 3	Off	Timed cycling: 60 min	Medium and quick 5	Timed cycling: 120 min	Strength training: 30 min	Flow 3	Timed cycling: 60 min	405	5-7
Week 4	Off	Strength training: 30 min	Timed cycling: 60 min	Long and steady 2	Timed cycling: 75 min	Short and fast 6	Timed cycling: 90 min	367	5-7

RUNNING PROGRAM: ENHANCE LEG SPEED AND PACE TO GO THE DISTANCE

As a full-body exercise, Nordic walking works many of the same muscles that running does. The upper and lower body move in opposition in both sports, but the range of motion for runners is much more limited. Instead, speed and pace create momentum and help runners go the distance.

The range of motion gained by Nordic walking and running can help you increase your running pace by extending stride length from the hip. Running with a greater range of motion enhances upper-body strength and flexibility, improving efficiency and running form. With the exception of the long levers, speed technique makes Nordic walking specifically helpful for runners.

Nordic walking has less momentum because it's a low-impact activity in which efforts are driven by muscle and power. That power translates into pure momentum on the running track. The stride mechanics and cardiorespiratory output of Nordic walking help runners go greater distances without perceiving effort. When the body is trained to operate on autopilot, distance becomes less challenging.

General Program Design

Objective: Enhance stride mechanics to increase pace and running speed. RPE fluctuates, but leg speed is the priority.

Frequency: Six times per week

Intensity: Mostly moderate to fast

Time (average): 60 to 75 minutes per workout

	Sun	Mon	Tue	Wed	Thu	Fri	Sat	Total time	RPE
Week 1	Off	Medium and steady 8	Strength training: 30 min	Timed run: 60 min	Short and fast 4	Boot camp 2	Timed run: 90 min	360	5-7
Week 2	Off	Strength training: 30 min	Timed run: 45 min	Flow 3	Free-style 1	Timed run: 90 min	Long and steady 5	420	6-7
Week 3	Off	Timed run: 60 min	Short and fast 5	Boot camp 1	Medium and quick 7	Strength training: 30 min	Timed run: 90 min	345	6-7
Week 4	Off	Short and fast 6	Timed run: 120 min	Strength training: 30 min	Flow 2	Timed run: 60 min	Boot camp 2	395	6-8

Note: See chapter 4 for information on speed technique for advanced cardio.

Although experts recommend that participation in your sport is really the best conditioning, sometimes specificity should take a back seat to the thing you love to do the most. Nordic walking is different from other cross-training activities because it has no weather limits. Rain, snow, or shine, you will never have to miss a workout because of weather. You can Nordic walk to cross-train any time.

CHAPTER 17

Customizing Your Program

This book provides programming ideas and structures in a variety of formats. Chapter 7 introduces the FITT principle of program design, with general recommendations based on skill and fitness level. Chapters 8 through 13 outline workouts relative to distance and intensity preferences. Chapters 15 and 16 describe ideas for exercise routines in terms of on long-term focus and goals. This chapter provides basic programming guidelines to ensure long-term success as you create your own program, discussing common hurdles and strategies for overcoming them. Finally, it highlights the principle of periodization and presents supplemental activities to enhance Nordic training.

Keys to a Successful Long-Term Training Program

Safe and sound physiological principles must be at the forefront of any program to ensure physical and mental enjoyment, improvement, and maintenance of results over time. The programs previously listed in this book contain the following principles. Consider incorporating them if you are customizing your own program.

Test and Retest

As chapter 7 discusses, when planning a program, you must determine your current level of fitness. The assessments provided (fitness assessment for walking health, 1-mile walking test) help to stratify you into the appropriate category. Use these assessments to determine a starting point that prevents you from either doing too much too soon or failing to sufficiently challenge yourself. This process is analogous to working with financial advisors. Upon first consultation, they never suggest that you immediately put your money into aggressive stock-market funds just because it sounds exciting (if so, find a new advisor fast). On the contrary, your current earnings and investments are assessed in conjunction with your short- and long-term goals to create a comprehensive strategy based on informed decisions. Similarly, fitness assessments provide critical information for planning both short-term and long-term goals. Retest every 4 to 6 weeks to get a good sense of your progress and to determine the next direction for your program.

Build Distance Gradually

Gradually increasing distance allows your body to adapt at its own rate while improving endurance, strength, and overall efficiency. Specifically, you should never increase your weekly distance by more than 10 percent. Doing too much too soon is a certain recipe for injury and burnout. The short-term gains may result in weeks of forced rest due to injury.

Fluctuate Intensity Daily

You should also select your intensity wisely, reevaluating it for each workout. High-intensity workouts performed back to back are not productive over time, leading to overuse injuries, restrictions of peak performance, and suppression of the immune system. As a rule of thumb, follow high-intensity workouts with routines of moderate or low intensity. Research suggests that consecutive workouts of high intensity (more than 80 percent HRmax) and long duration (more than 90 minutes) can suppress the immune system for up to three days, making you more susceptible to infections of the upper respiratory tract. On the contrary, regular bouts of moderate intensity (65 to 80 percent HRmax) and duration (<90 minutes) positively boost the immune system. Therefore, alternate the intensities of your workouts throughout the week to heighten your performance, keep your routine interesting and motivating, and build a strong immune system.

Respect Rest Days

Many athletes have a hard time taking a day off from exercise, perhaps for fear that they will lose their edge. However, rest days are one of the most critical parts of any training program. Relax in the knowledge that your body appreciates the break. Time off allows the body to repair itself, grow stronger, and return to the next workout with vigor.

How to Stay on Track or Get Back on Track

People have the best intentions when it comes to exercising regularly. Most understand the clear benefits and try hard to balance everyday demands with what they know to be good for them. The trick is maintaining an exercise routine when, despite motivation and good intentions, life seems to get in the way. If you are one of the unique few who has it all figured out, please consider writing a book about it for those who have difficulty juggling life and exercise. Here are some of the common obstacles to regular exercise.

Injuries

Injuries are the nemesis of many athletes, while others seldom even get a hangnail. Regardless of your disposition, you should be mindful of techniques for preventing injury, as well as of smart plans that help you recover when injured.

First and foremost, you must listen to your body when aches and pains are present. The body is remarkable at telling us things we need to know. We just need to learn to pay attention. Drop the intensity or duration of your training if you feel exhausted or if you have muscle or joint pain. You may just need a day off. However, if discomfort persists for a few weeks, seek professional care to identify the underlying cause. To prevent injury, plan a workout routine that does not force you to do too much too soon. You must alternate the intensity of your workouts, rather than performing hard workouts back to back. This gives your body the time it needs to mend and repair itself.

On the other hand, if you are injured, you must listen to the advice of your physical therapist or doctor. Most advise that you gradually work back up to full speed. Take heed and listen to your body! You may benefit from other exercises, such as swimming or yoga, which minimize the stress on a particular area. You cannot live by the mantra "No pain, no gain" if you want to recover quickly. Sleep is also a critical piece of injury recovery and prevention. A myriad of repair processes take place during sleep, so be sure to get the amount that your body craves. Overall, be patient and have faith that respecting your limitations will help you enjoy Nordic walking in the long run.

Weather

The great benefit of Nordic walking is that it is intended to be performed outside in the fresh air, ideally in scenic settings where you can look around and enjoy your surroundings. For this reason, many outdoor enthusiasts are drawn to Nordic walking. Unfortunately, Nordic walkers are beholden to the weather. Take note of the recommendations in chapter 2 and be sure to wear proper clothing for anticipated weather conditions. If severe adverse weather is forecast, stay out of the elements. Don't compromise your safety for the sake of a workout! To ensure that you maintain progress with your training, use a treadmill or an elliptical trainer as a short-term alternative. On the other hand, if you thrive on training in rain, sleet, hail, or snow, then more power to you!

Work and Family Commitments

Balancing work, personal pursuits, and family can be a challenge for many. How can you focus on one activity without compromising the quality of all the others? The beauty of Nordic walking is that it encourages socializing. You can Nordic walk side by side with your family and friends for a simultaneous experience of fun and fitness. Exercising with coworkers both relieves stress and promotes team building. Even if your skill level differs from your partner's, you can increase the intensity of your workout by modifying tip resistance. These workouts can count as low-intensity days, which are an important part of any weekly routine.

Overtraining

Even if you don't exercise six or seven days per week, you may still be prone to overtraining. Overtraining can also result from lack of rest between workouts, lack of sleep, and consecutive high-intensity workouts. Because everyone is built differently, learn to recognize the signals that your body gives you. Signs of overtraining include chronic muscle soreness, insomnia, chronic fatigue, lack of appetite, depression, frequent sickness, increase in injuries, irritability, lack of interest in activity, and decreased performance. If you experience these symptoms, you must decrease the intensity and duration of your routine until symptoms subside. When you feel better, reexamine your routine to ensure it is balanced and allows for proper recovery.

Periodization Training

Periodization is a training method characterized by manipulating exercise volume, intensity, and technique typically over a year of training (*macrocycle*) in order to promote optimal performance. The training period can then be divided into shorter cycles called *mesocycles* or *microcyles* in order to accomplish short- and long-term goals without injury or overtraining. Figure 17.1 shows how the preparatory period begins the training cycle with high training volume, moderate intensity, and minimal focus on technique. During the transition phase, volume and intensity are both at moderate levels. During the competition period, the relationship between volume and intensity is reversed; volume decreases while intensity and technique increase. This cycle produces peaks in sport performance.

Typically, this method trains athletes for a specific event, but it can also be used for maintaining motivation and a high level of performance. Use this training schedule as a guide rather than as a hard and fast rule. For example, you may want to spend an extra week on the preparatory section if you don't feel ready to begin increasing intensity. Individuals vary in how quickly they adapt to exercise, so you should always listen to your body when making changes. The following information provides an overview of the training philosophy.

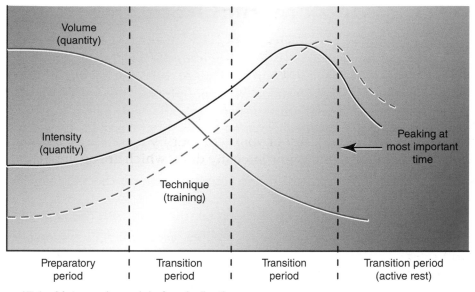

Figure 17.1   Matveyev's model of periodization.
Adapted from L. Matveyev, 1965, *Periodization of sports training* (Moscow: Izdatelstvo Fizkultura i Sport).

- *Preparatory period.* The first phase of the program establishes a base level of cardiorespiratory endurance by coupling a moderate-to-high level of volume with low-intensity exercise. This helps the aerobic energy system more efficiently use oxygen and gives muscles, tendons, and ligaments time to adjust. This aspect of periodization regulates the pace to minimize the risk of injuries. Depending on your fitness level, this period can take one to two months as you establish a solid foundation and prepare your body for more intense challenges.

- *Transition period.* The transition period is meant to ease the shift from the high-volume training of the preparatory period to the high-intensity training of the competition period. During this period, focus on developing strength and speed with sport-specific movements. Since volume and intensity are equally challenging, you must take days off for adequate rest and recovery.

- *Competition period.* This period can last anywhere from several weeks to several months, depending on the season of your chosen sport. The low-volume, high-intensity workouts help you peak for competition without overtraining. However, you can also use this period for maintenance if there are multiple events within a few weeks. In this case, the volume and intensity should remain moderate. In general, this period should last no more than two or three weeks.

- *Active rest.* The second transition period, also known as active rest, provides a mental and physical break. This period can last between one and four weeks. Use moderate activity to prevent deconditioning. Once you have recovered, you can return to the preparatory period to resume the periodization cycle.

Supplemental Activities

Participation in other sports can provide a welcome reprieve from daily Nordic walking. Many popular sports even enhance Nordic walking fitness. Note that sports don't need to look like Nordic walking to provide benefits, which is the beauty and function of cross-training. Many people fear they will lose their edge if they deviate from the activities of their particular sport on a weekly basis. On the contrary, cross-training provides both a mental and physical vacation from the primary exercise, which heightens motivation and performance in the long run. Generally speaking, if you are not competing in a Nordic walking event, then cross-training with other activities several days a week can be beneficial for your training cycle.

If you are training for a Nordic walking competition with the periodization method, the preparatory period is a great time to supplement alternate activities. During this period, sport-specific technique is not essential. Instead, focus on increasing your general base of cardiorespiratory fitness. However, as you progress through the stages of transition and competition, stick to Nordic walking to work toward your peak.

Resistance Training

If performed appropriately, resistance training can be an asset to overall performance of any activity by enhancing strength, endurance, and power. Similar to the discussion in chapter 7 with cardiovascular endurance training, you must choose an appropriate rate of exercise progression with resistance training to ensure desired improvements are achieved and that health issues and injuries do not arise. The following information provides guidelines for optimal resistance training progression, also known as the FITT Principle.

- *Frequency.* In order to improve and maintain muscle fitness the recommendation is to resistance train 2 to 3 days per week. As an option, these sessions can be done by working all the major muscle groups 2 to 3 days a week in longer sessions, or broken up into 3 to 5 days a week of shorter sessions using fewer muscle groups. Regardless of which schedule is chosen, there should be a 48 hour rest period between working any particular muscle group. Beginning Nordic walkers who are working on skill development should aim for at least 2 days per week, but those who are working on fitness proficiency and competition may resistance train between 3 to 5 days each week. Muscle fitness gains can be maintained if training muscle groups 1 day a week considering the intensity remains the same.

- *Intensity.* Defined by volume, intensity can be measured collectively by the amount of weight lifted by the number of repetitions performed. To improve muscular strength and endurance, 8 to 12 repetitions are ideal with an amount of weight that elicits fatigue or approximately 60%-80% of effort. Two to four sets should be the goal, with each set bringing about fatigue rather than muscle failure. Nordic walkers who are working on skill development should aim for performing 2 to 3 sets of 8 to 12 repetitions, while those in the other two categories should aim for a 3 to 4 sets of 10 to 15 repetitions.

• *Time*. Relative to resistance training, time pertains to how long it takes to perform an exercise, as well as how long it takes to perform a workout. Although there is not an exact amount of time to perform exercises, they should be done in a controlled manner that is focused on technique with a breathing pattern that results in exhaling during the lifting phase and inhaling during the lowering phase. In between sets, a rest period of 2 to 3 minutes should be observed if doing a strength or endurance routine. Generally, the higher intensity the routine the longer the rest period should be. A workout session can last between 20 and 60 minutes depending on the desired intensity and number of exercises being performed.

• *Type*. A complete resistance training program should include 8 to 10 multi-joint exercises that include more than one muscle group. In addition to traditional weights, other types of resistance training techniques may include machines, resistance bands, and body weight. For those training for a competition or event, the type of exercises chosen is important. As discussed in the transition phase of periodization, when the competition or event draws closer choose strength exercises that closely resemble the exercise you are training for.

In order to continue to show improvements in muscular fitness, progressive overload is an essential component. This requires continuously challenging the muscles by increasing the amount of weight being used, the number of repetitions per set (without exceeding > 12 repetitions), or more frequently training the muscle groups.

In-Line Skating

The in-line skating stride is rhythmic in nature and involves long arm and leg levers that are similar to those used in Nordic walking. This coordinated movement engages similar muscle groups, including the pectorals, deltoids, latissimi dorsi, abdominal muscles, hip flexors, quadriceps, and gluteal muscles. This minimal-impact activity is a perfect option for diversifying your training once or twice a week. It also enhances cardiorespiratory fitness.

Cross-Country Skiing

Nordic walking is often compared with cross-country skiing because both activities involve contralateral movements of upper and lower body and poles. One of the significant differences between the activities is that cross-country skiers glide between strides. However, both activities use similar muscle groups, so they are highly compatible in terms of cross-training during the off season. Cross-country skiing is very demanding, so Nordic walkers should gradually introduce it into their schedules, allowing adequate rest days to limit overuse injuries.

Swimming

Exercising in the water has very little impact on your joints. For this reason, swimming is an excellent cross-training tool for virtually any activity since it minimizes overuse injuries. Since swimming uses all the major muscle groups, it is a perfect complement to Nordic walking that provides a distinct diversion from land-based activity and maintains fitness gains.

Index

Note: The italicized *t* and *f* following page numbers refer to tables and figures, respectively.

A

accelerometers 20-21
accessories 20*f*-21
active rest 199
adaptation 187
advanced cardio training. *See also* cardiorespiratory fitness
    about 3, 4-6, 38-39
    drills 39-43, 40*f*, 41*f*, 42*f*
aerobic conditioning 4-6
age 110
agility
    about 6-7, 8, 79
    drills 80*f*-82*f*
alpine skiing 190*t*
altitude, exercising at 106
American College of Sports Medicine (ACSM) 23
anaerobic conditioning 4-6, 38
apparel 18-19, 98-99, 105
Aquaclips 98-99
arm movement 26, 28*f*
assessment of skill and fitness
    about 109, 112
    1-Mile Walking Test 113*f*
    questionnaire 110-112
    retesting 196
asthma 106

B

Back and Shoulders, stretch for 92*f*
Back Extensions 55*f*
Back of Arms, stretch for 95*f*
Back of Lower Leg, stretch for 96*f*
Back of Thigh, stretch for 93*f*
backpacking 190*t*
backpacks 20, 99
Backside Kickers 85*f*
Backside Strength 50*f*-51
back strength 2, 3
balance 3, 6, 8, 198
balance and coordination
    about 73
    drills 74*f*-79, 75*f*, 76*f*, 77*f*, 78*f*
baskets, pole 13
belt packs 20
body awareness 3, 6, 73, 79-80, 158
bone density 2, 3, 4
bowling 190*t*

C

CamelBaks 98-99
cardiorespiratory fitness. *See also* advanced cardio training
    about 3, 4-6, 38, 110, 170

assessing 168
competitive programs 170-171
fitness proficiency programs 170-171
results of improved 168*t*
skill development programs 168
cardiovascular endurance progression 112-113
Chest Stretch 91*f*
circuit training
    about 154-156
    boot-camp workouts 163-165
    components of 159
    flow workouts 166-168
    freestyle workouts 160-162
    terrain assessment 160
Classic Push-Ups With a Twist 59*f*
clothing 17-18, 98-99, 105
cold weather 99, 105-106
competition period 198
competition training category
    about 108
    for cardiorespiratory fitness 170-173
    for total-body fitness 179-180
conditioning programs
    about 37-38
    advanced cardio training 38-43, 40*f*, 41*f*, 42*f*
    lower-body strength training 43-57
    power training 63-71
    upper-body strength training 57-62
Continuous and Dynamic Walking Lunges 88*f*
contract-relax stretching technique 119*f*
Controlled Jousting 76*f*
cool-down 80, 118-120, 119*f*, 160
Coolmax fabric 19
coordination 7
core strength drills 52*f*-57*f*, 53*f*, 54*f*, 55*f*, 56*f*, 57*f*
cross-country skiing 190*t*, 201-202
Crossover Walk 82*f*
cross-training
    cross-country skiing 191-192
    cycling 192-193
    Outdoor Cross-Training program 157
    principles 186-191
    running 193-194
Cupping for Grip Development progression 29*f*
cycling 190*t*, 192-193

D

Developing Stride Length progression 31*f*
distance, weekly 196
Double Poling 61*f*
downhill terrain 101*f*-102
dynamic flexibility drills 83*f*-88*f*
dynamic stretching 117

E
easy workouts, short 126-128*t*, 129-132
elbows 35
endorphins 3
equestrian 190*t*
equipment
   about 9-10
   accessories 20*f*-21
   apparel 18-19*f*
   poles 11*f*-16, 11*f*, 12*f*
   shoes 17-18*f*
   weather and terrain considerations 98-99

F
fabrics, clothing 18-19
fartlek 158
fitness, full-body. *See also* conditioning programs
   about 3, 179-180
   competitive programs 184-185
   fitness proficiency programs 182-184
   skill development programs 180-182
fitness proficiency training category
   about 108-109
   for cardiorespiratory fitness 175-176
   for total-body fitness 182-184
FITT principle 113-115, 200-201
flexibility
   about 82-83
   dynamic drills 83*f*-88*f*
   stationary drills 89*f*-97*f*
Foot and Ankle Rolls 45*f*
foot contact 36
footwear 17-18*f*
footwork 79
Forward Bend 90*f*
Forward Bounding 67*f*
Forward Leaps 68*f*-69
Forward Leg Lifts 87*f*
frequency, of exercise 115
Front of Lower Leg, stretch for 97*f*
Front of Thigh, stretch for 92-93*f*
Front Press With Partner 57*f*

G
gait 23
gear. *See* equipment
gloves 19*f*
golf 190*t*
GPS devices 21, 120
grip development 29*f*, 35-36

H
handle, pole 10*f*, 16, 29*f*, 34*f*
Handle Release progression 34*f*
heart health 3
heart rate
   about 39
   heart rate monitors 20*f*-21, 122
   heart-rate reserve (HHR) 121-123
   maximum heart rate 115, 121
heat 98-99, 104-105
heel pain 18
height, pole 14-15, 23
hiking 190*t*
hills 37, 100*f*-102, 101*f*

Hill Training 41*f*-42
hold-relax stretching technique 118, 119*f*
hold-relax with agonistic contraction stretching
         technique 119*f*-120
HRmax 115, 121
hydration 20, 98-99, 104-105, 106
hypothermia 105, 106

I
ice 99
illness 110
impact modifications 64-65
improvement stage 123-124
initiation stage 123
injuries
   dealing with 197
   injury prevention 23-25, 35-36, 114
   pole height and 15
   power training 63-64
   repetitive use 22, 23-24
   in self-assessment 110
injury rehabilitation 3
in-line skating 190*t*, 201
Inner Thigh, stretch for 94*f*-95
intensity, of exercise 115, 121-123*t*, 196
interval training 6, 38

J
joints, impact on 4

K
Kahtoola Microspikes 99
Kamikaze Uphill program 100
Karvonen's method 121-122
Knee Lifts 86*f*

L
leaning back 34
Leg Swings 84*f*
limbering 116
long and steady workouts
   about 151-152*t*
   workouts 153-156
Long Arms progression 28*f*
Long Legs progression 30*f*
Lowa 17
lower-body
   strength training 44-51*f*, 45*f*, 46*f*, 47*f*, 48*f*, 49*f*, 50*f*
   technique progressions 29*f*-31*f*
Lunges 47*f*

M
maintenance stage 124
mall walking 98
maximum heart rate 115, 122
medium and quick workouts
   about 139-140*t*
   workouts 141-144
medium and steady workouts
   about 133-134*t*
   workouts 135-138
mobility 3
movement efficiency 7
Multidirectional Arm Raises 61-62*f*
Multidirectional Leg Lifts 49*f*

muscle endurance 3, 6
muscle memory 80
muscle strength 3, 7-8

N
Nordic walking
    about 2-3, 22-23
    advantages 3-8
    assessing skill and fitness levels 109-114, 113*ft*
    fitness and athletic benefits 4-8
    health benefits 3-4
    skill development 23-25
    skill levels 108-109
    technique progressions 24-36
    vs. trekking 102-103
nutrition 105

O
Old-Fashioned Squats 46*f*
Old-Fashioned Step-Ups With Bench 51*f*
1-Mile Walking Test 113*f*
Opposing Arm and Leg Raises 56*f*
outdoor circuit training
    about 158-160
    boot-camp workouts 164-166
    components of 160
    flow workouts 165-168
    freestyle workouts 160-162
    terrain assessment 160
Outdoor Cross-Training 158
Outer Thigh, stretch for 94*f*
Overhead Lateral Stretch 89*f*
overload 187
overtraining 198

P
pace 24-25, 120*t*
pain management 3
Partner Choo-Choo Train 77*f*
Partner Mirroring 75*f*
pedometers 20
perceived exertion, rating of 122-123*t*
periodization, of training 198-199*f*
physical therapy 23
plantar fasciitis 18
plyometrics 161
PNF stretching 118-120, 117*f*
Polates 98
poles, Nordic walking
    about 9-10
    adjustable length 13-14
    baskets 13
    cleaning 16-17
    costs 10
    fixed length 13-14
    handle 10*f*
    height 14-15, 23
    maintenance 14-15
    shaft 13
    tips 12-13*f*
    vs. trekking 102-103
    weight 20
    wrist straps 11-12*f*
poles, trekking 9
postural development 2

posture, Nordic walking 25-26
Power Skips 70-71*f*
power-training
    about 7-8, 63-65
    drills 65*f*-71*f,* 66*f,* 67*f,* 68*f,* 69*f*
preparatory period 199
proprioceptors 82

R
range of motion, enhanced 6
rating of perceived exertion (RPE) 122-123*t*
Reebok 17
Resistance Rotation With Partner 54*f*
resistance training 200-202
rest days 196
resting heart rate 121-122
resting pulse rate 111
rhythm and cadence workout 168-169
Running 42*f*-43
running 193*t,* 196-197
running shoes 17

S
safety guidelines
    about 103, 106-107
    cold and wind 99, 105-106
    heat 98-99, 104-105
    at high altitude 106
sequential learning 24
shaft, pole 12, 16
shoes 17-18*f*
short and easy workouts
    about 126-128*t*
    workouts 129-132
short and fast workouts
    about 145-146*t*
    workouts 147-150
sidewalks 106
Single-Side Agility 81*f*
Single-Side Balance Awareness 74*f*
Single-Side Squats 48*f*
skating, in-line 192*t,* 201
skill development training category
    about 108
    for cardiorespiratory fitness 175-176
    for total-body fitness 182-184
skill levels 108-109
smoking 111
snow and ice 99
snowshoeing 189*t*
snowshoes 99
soccer 192*t*
socks 18
specificity, sport 187-191, 190*t*
speed 120
Spine and Pelvic Rotation progression 32*f*
sports
    categories of 190
    chart of 192*t*
    compatibility with Nordic walking 190-193
    and cross-training 188-189
SpringBoost 17
Squat Thrusts 69*f*-70
stability 3
Standing Rotations 52*f*

static stretching 117
stationary flexibility drills 89*f*-97*f*
Stationary Jumps 65*f*-66
steady workouts
    long 151-152*t*, 153-156
    medium 133-134*t*, 135-138
Step-Ups on a Curb 80*f*
strength. *See* muscle *strength*
strength training
    about 43-44
    core strength drills 52*f*-57*f*, 53*f*, 54*f*, 55*f*, 56*f*
    lower-body drills 44-51*f*, 45*f*, 46*f*, 47*f*, 48*f*, 49*f*, 50*f*
    resistance training 200-202
    upper-body drills 57-62*f*, 58*f*, 59*f*, 60*f*, 61*f*
stress reduction 4
stress-reduction walk 167
Stretch for Back and Shoulders 92*f*
Stretch for Back of Arms 95*f*
Stretch for Back of Lower Leg 96*f*
Stretch for Back of Thigh 93*f*
Stretch for Chest 91*f*
Stretch for Lower Back and Hamstrings 90*f*
Stretch for Front of Lower Leg 97*f*
Stretch for Front of Thigh 92-93*f*
Stretch for Inner Thigh 94*f*-95
Stretch for Outer Thigh 94*f*
Stretch for Obliques and Back 89*f*
stretching
    dynamic flexibility drills 86*f*-88*f*
    stationary flexibility drills 89*f*-97*f*
    warm-up 116-126, 117*f*
striding 23, 26-29*f*, 27*f*, 28*f*, 36, 37
swimming 190*t*, 202
Synchronized Walking 78*f*
synthetic fabrics 105

T
technique progressions
    common errors 34-36
    complex 32*f*-34*f*, 33*f*
    lower-body 29*f*-31*f*, 30*f*
    pace 24-25
    upper-body 25*f*-29*f*, 26*f*, 27*f*, 28*f*
terrain
    in circuit training 160
    downhill 101*f*-102
    equipment selection and 98-99
    selection 99
    uphill 100*f*-101
time, of exercise 115
Tip Engagement progression 33*f*
tips, pole 12-13*f*, 16, 25, 33*f*, 36, 102-103
tip-to-grip biofeedback 103
torso rotation 32*f*, 35
total-body fitness. *See also* conditioning programs
    about 3, 181-182
    competitive programs 184-185
    fitness proficiency programs 182-184
    skill development programs 180-182
training programs. *See also* workouts
    competition training category 109, 175-176, 184-185
    fitness proficiency training category 108-109, 175-176, 182-184
    long-term success 197-200

    periodization 198-199
    skill development training category 108, 175-176, 182-184
    supplemental activities 200-202
transition period 199
treadmills 98, 197
trekking 102-103, 192*t*
trekking poles 8, 103
Triceps Press 60*f*
Tuck Jumps 66*f*
Turbo Walking 40*f*-41
type, of exercise 115

U
Underhand Rows 58*f*
uphill terrain 100*f*-101
upper-body
    strength training 57-62*f*, 58*f*, 59*f*, 60*f*, 61*f*
    technique progressions 25*f*-29*f*, 26*f*, 27*f*, 28*f*

V
visual skills 6

W
Walk and Swing progression 27*f*
walking 190*t*
Walking Backward 79
walking meditation 167-168
warm-ups 116-118, 117*f*, 159
water bottles 20
weather
    and clothing 19
    cold and wind 99, 105-106
    equipment and clothing 98-99, 197
    heat 98-99, 104-105
    and injury prevention 46
weight 110-111
weight loss 3
wicking clothing 105
wind 106
Woodchoppers 53*f*
work, and exercise 197
workouts
    boot-camp workouts 163-165
    choosing right 113-114
    components of safe 159
    cool-down 118-120, 119*f*
    cross-training 188-196
    FITT principle 114-115
    flow workouts 165-168
    freestyle workouts 160-162
    long and steady 151-152*t*, 153-156
    medium and quick 139-140*t*, 141-144
    medium and steady 133-134*t*, 135-138
    pace and intensity 120*t*-123*t*
    progression of routines 123-124
    short and easy 126-128*t*, 129-132
    short and fast 145-146*t*, 147-150
    training program success 195-202
    warm-ups 116-118, 117*f*
wrists 35
wrist straps, pole 11-12*f*

Y
yoga 190*t*

About the Authors

Suzanne Nottingham is known worldwide as one of the top sport and fitness instructors with more than 25 years of experience in marketing, programming, and education. She has been a Nordic walking instructor since 2001 and is past director of North American Nordic walking education for Leki USA. Her work has been pivotal in launching Nordic walking in North America.

In 2006 she created and launched the Nordic Walk Now Instructor Training Program and the Walk To Live Workshop to educate the public about safety, skills and equipment. To date, she and her team of 21 education leaders have trained more than 450 instructors and community advocates in North America. New in January 2010 is Nordic Walk Now's Instructor Training extension program, Master Fitness, an eight hour athletic training course. Her Web site at www.nordicwalknow.com is a portal for instructors and the public.

Since 1990, Nottingham has been a spokesperson and continuing education provider for the American Council on Exercise (ACE), and she was on the California Governor's Council on Physical Fitness and Sports. In 2000, she received the fitness industry's highest honor as IDEA's Fitness Instructor of the Year. In her spare time, Suzanne volunteers as an educator for Disabled Sports East Sierra for winter and summer sports, the Wounded Warrior Program, and No Barriers, the United States' premier event for disabled athletic-minded people. But she claims her real job is as a ski instructor at Mammoth Mountain Ski Resort in California, where she has lived since 1980.

Nottingham is also the author of Fitness In-Line Skating (Human Kinetics, 1997) and is known as one of the pioneers in the launch and success of in-line skating in the United States.

Alexandra Jurasin has been in the health, fitness, and wellness field for over 15 years and is a national lead instructor trainer for Nordic Walk Now teaching instructors and classes at conferences throughout the United States. Jurasin has designed and managed fitness and wellness programs for more than 50 corporations and police and fire departments throughout California, and she has been a guest speaker at national and international conferences. She has served on the faculty in the health science and kinesiology departments at California State University at Fullerton and Santa Ana College in Southern California and was recently the general manager of the Google G-Fit Fitness Centers. Currently Jurasin works for Plus One Health Management as the account executive for Amgen's national fitness and wellness programs, and she is a contributing author to the American College of Sports Medicine text for personal training.

Jurasin received a bachelor's degree in exercise physiology from the University of San Francisco, where she also competed in basketball, and a master's degree in kinesiology from California State University at Fullerton. She holds multiple health and fitness certifications, including recognition as an ACE Academy instructor.

Jurasin has a passion for all outdoor activities, where she derives inspiration and motivation in nature. In addition to Nordic walking, she enjoys cycling, hiking, camping, and any new life adventure.